The Smile of Horror

When the Laughter Dies

Heinrich Wilson

Heinrich Wilson Publishing

Contents

Foreword

There is something deeply wrong with clowns.

You've felt it, haven't you? That small tightening in your chest when you see one at a distance. The instinctive step backward when a painted face turns toward you. The way your smile freezes when a clown approaches, their grin wide and fixed, their eyes unreadable beneath layers of white greasepaint and exaggerated color.

We tell ourselves it's silly. Clowns are for children's parties. They're harmless entertainers, relics of circus tents and balloon animals. They exist to make us laugh, to bring joy. That's what we're supposed to believe.

But somewhere deep in our evolutionary wiring, something screams a warning. Something ancient and primal recognizes the threat hidden beneath the costume. This book is not about overcoming your fear of clowns. This book is about understanding why that fear is justified.

The clown, as we know it today, is a relatively recent invention. Yet the archetype is far older: the trickster, the fool, the figure who exists outside normal social rules. Every culture has one. The court jester who could mock the king. The shaman who wore masks to commune with spirits. The sacred clown of indigenous tribes who violated taboos to teach lessons. These figures were powerful precisely because they were dangerous. They operated in the spaces between order and chaos, between the sacred and the profane.

But something changed. Somewhere in the evolution from sacred fool to circus performer, the clown lost its holy terror and gained something worse: a manufactured cheerfulness that feels fundamentally dishonest. The modern clown isn't dangerous in the way a warrior is dangerous. The modern clown is dangerous the way a broken machine is dangerous, something that should function one way but has gone catastrophically wrong.

Consider the basic construction of a clown. The face is painted in stark, unnatural colors. White greasepaint obliterates individual features, creating a blank canvas. On this canvas, new features are drawn in grotesque exaggeration. The mouth becomes enormous, stretched into a permanent grin that shows too many teeth. The eyes are circled in black or red, making them appear sunken and hollow. Tears are painted below the eyes, suggesting sadness beneath the forced smile. The nose, that ridiculous red ball, draws attention to the center of the face but offers nothing human to focus on.

This is a mask made of paint, destroying the face beneath while pretending to enhance it. And masks, throughout human history, have always been objects of power and fear. They allow the wearer to shed their humanity and take on a different identity. When you look at a clown, you're not seeing a person. You're seeing a construct, and you have no idea what is hiding underneath.

The costume completes the transformation. Oversized shoes force an awkward, lurching gait. Clothing violates the expected proportions of a human body, either too large or too small. Bright, clashing colors signal danger in the same way poisonous insects signal danger. Ruffles and bells and pompoms make the clown seem simultaneously childish and ancient, innocent and corrupt.

Then there's the behavior. Clowns invade your space without permission. They make loud noises, sudden movements. They violate every unspoken rule of social interaction with gleeful abandon. The unpredictability is the point. The loss of control is the point. In any other context, we would recognize this as predatory behavior. We would back away. We would protect our children.

But clowns are supposed to be fun, so we override our instincts. We force ourselves to smile back. We let our children be lifted into the air by someone whose face we cannot read. We pretend everything is fine.

Until it isn't.

John Wayne Gacy understood this better than anyone. He knew that the clown costume provided perfect camouflage. Who would suspect Pogo the Clown, the friendly entertainer at children's parties, of being a serial killer? Who would question the man in the rainbow wig and painted smile? Gacy buried thirty-three bodies beneath his house while maintaining his double life as a beloved community figure. The clown wasn't just a hobby for him. It was a hunting strategy.

Gacy was not an anomaly. He was a revelation. He showed us what we already suspected deep down: that the painted smile could hide anything. That the costume designed to bring joy could just as easily conceal monstrosity. That our instinctive fear of clowns was not irrational at all, but a survival mechanism we had foolishly learned to ignore.

Popular culture caught up quickly. Within years of Gacy's arrest, Stephen King published "It," giving us Pennywise the Dancing Clown. Not coincidentally, King has stated that his own fear of clowns predated Gacy but was crystallized by him. The novel tapped into something primal and widespread: the understanding that clowns are not what they pretend to be, that beneath the makeup lies something we should fear.

Since then, the killer clown has become one of horror's most enduring archetypes. The Joker evolved from comic book villain to philosophical monster. Art the Clown traumatized audiences with silent, sadistic glee. Twisty brought tragedy and terror to American Horror Story. The 2016 clown sightings turned fiction into reality, with communities worldwide genuinely terrified of figures lurking in woods and under streetlights.

That 2016 incident deserves particular attention because it revealed something crucial about our relationship with clowns. When reports began surfacing of people dressed as clowns appearing in unexpected places (woods, parking lots, street corners at night), the response was immediate and visceral. Police departments were flooded with calls. Schools went into lockdown. Parents kept children home. Armed citizens formed patrols. Social media exploded with warnings, sightings, and rapidly escalating fear.

The rational response would have been laughter. These were obviously pranks, hoaxes, attempts at viral fame. No actual violence had occurred in most cases. The "clowns" were typically just people in costumes, standing around looking creepy. But rationality had nothing to do with the response. Communities reacted as if under genuine threat, because on some fundamental level, the threat felt real.

This is what makes clowns unique among our cultural fears. We don't react this way to most costumes. A person in a werewolf mask might startle us, but we don't call the police. Someone dressed as a zombie at the wrong time of year might seem odd, but we don't organize armed patrols. Yet clowns in unexpected contexts trigger a response usually reserved for actual predators. Why?

The answer lies in what clowns represent: deception at its most fundamental level. Everything about a clown is a lie. The smile is painted on, incapable of changing. The cheerfulness is manufactured, performed on command regardless of actual emotion. The costume obscures the human form. The makeup obliterates individual features. You cannot read a clown's true intentions, mood, or thoughts. You cannot predict their behavior. You cannot see the person underneath.

In evolutionary terms, this is catastrophically dangerous. Humans are social animals who survive through cooperation, and cooperation requires the ability to read others. We assess trustworthiness through facial expressions, body language, eye contact, and countless other subtle cues. A clown destroys all of these. The painted face provides no useful information. The exaggerated costume makes body language meaningless. The performance creates a wall between the performer and the audience that cannot be penetrated.

This is why children often cry when confronted with clowns. They haven't yet learned to suppress their survival instincts. They see what adults have trained themselves to ignore: a figure that mimics humanity while being fundamentally inhuman. The clown moves like a person but doesn't look like one. It speaks but the mouth doesn't match the words. It smiles but the smile never changes. Children recognize this as wrong, as threatening, as something to flee from.

Adults know better, of course. We understand that clowns are just performers doing a job. We've been socialized to associate them with birthdays, circuses, and harmless fun. We override our instincts because society tells us to. But the instincts don't disappear. They wait beneath the surface, ready to explode when the context shifts even slightly. Put that same clown in the woods at midnight instead of a birthday party at noon, and suddenly everyone agrees: this is a threat.

The clown has become our modern boogeyman for good reason. It embodies anxieties that are increasingly relevant in contemporary life. We live in an age of performance, where everyone curates a public persona that may bear little resemblance to their private self. Social media has turned us all into performers, carefully constructing images of happiness, success, and fulfillment that may be completely false. We present smiling faces to the world while hiding depression, anger, desperation, or worse.

The clown is the ultimate symbol of this phenomenon. It is pure performance with no authentic core. It exists only to be looked at, to generate a specific emotional response, to fulfill a role. What the performer actually feels is irrelevant. The show must go on. The smile must remain. And we can never know what lies beneath.

This is why clowns translate so effectively into horror. They're already horrifying. The horror genre simply makes explicit what was always implicit. When Pennywise promises "you'll float too," he's not transforming from something innocent into something evil. He's revealing the evil that was always there, hidden beneath the costume and the carnival music. When the Joker explains his scars with contradictory stories, he's demonstrating the fundamental unknowability that makes all clowns unsettling. When Art the Clown commits his atrocities in silence, he's showing us that the painted smile means nothing, conceals everything, and promises only pain.

The history of clowns is not a story of innocent entertainers corrupted by pop culture. It's a story of dangerous figures who were always dangerous, who existed on society's margins precisely because they violated its norms. The sacred clowns of indigenous cultures were holy terrors who broke taboos to teach lessons. The court jesters wielded their mockery like weapons. The Harlequins and Pierrots of European tradition carried undertones of melancholy, chaos, and barely restrained violence.

Modern clowns inherited this legacy but lost the cultural framework that made it acceptable. They became sanitized, commercialized, reduced to birthday party entertainment. But the danger didn't disappear. It went underground, waiting for the right moment to resurface. Gacy gave it permission. Stephen King gave it a name. And an entire generation of horror creators has been exploring its depths ever since.

This book will trace that evolution. We'll examine the psychology behind our fear, the cultural history that shaped it, and the killers (both real and fictional) who embodied it. We'll look at how clowns became symbols of chaos in an ordered world, of deception in an age demanding authenticity, of violence hidden behind a smile.

By the time you finish reading, you won't see clowns the same way. You'll understand that your fear is not a weakness to overcome but a strength to embrace. You'll recognize the painted smile for what it truly is: a mask that hides monsters, a lie that promises nothing, and a warning we should never have learned to ignore.

The clown's greatest trick was convincing us it was harmless. This book will show you the truth that was always there, hiding behind the greasepaint and the grin.

Welcome to the smile of horror.

Chapter One

The Painted Smile: A Cultural Phenomenon

The smile is humanity's most universal gesture. Across cultures, across continents, across the entire span of human history, the smile communicates joy, friendliness, welcome. It's one of the first expressions babies learn to recognize. It's one of the last things we lose when dementia steals everything else. The smile is coded into our DNA as a signal of safety, of benign intent, of shared humanity.

So what happens when that signal lies?

The painted smile of a clown is perhaps the most disturbing inversion of human expression ever created. It takes our most fundamental gesture of trust and transforms it into something unreadable, unchanging, and ultimately meaningless. A real smile involves the entire face. The eyes crinkle. The cheeks rise. Tiny muscles around the mouth engage in ways we're not even consciously aware of. These microexpressions allow us to distinguish genuine happiness from polite performance, authentic joy from social obligation.

But a clown's smile is painted on. It never changes. It remains frozen whether the clown is happy or miserable, friendly or homicidal, celebrating or grieving. You cannot read emotion in a painted smile. You cannot judge intent. The smile becomes a wall between you and whatever human (if anything human remains) exists beneath the makeup.

This violation of our most basic social signal is not accidental. It's the entire point of the clown's construction. The clown exists to unsettle, even when it's supposedly entertaining. It operates in the space between human and inhuman, between friend and threat, between laughter and terror. The painted smile is the gateway to that space.

To understand how we arrived at this cultural moment, where clowns have become synonymous with horror, we need to trace the evolution of the clown through history. The figure we recognize today is a relatively recent invention, but its roots stretch back thousands of years to the very origins of performance and ritual.

The earliest clowns were not entertainers in any modern sense. They were sacred figures, operating at the boundaries of the spiritual world. Indigenous cultures across North America had sacred clown societies whose members performed crucial religious functions. These clowns (the Heyoka of the Lakota, the Koshare of the Pueblo peoples, the Newekwe of the Zuni) did not make people laugh for entertainment. They violated taboos, performed acts considered obscene or dangerous, and spoke truths that could not otherwise be voiced.

A sacred clown might walk backward, speak in opposites, or deliberately do everything wrong. They might mock authority figures, break social norms, or engage in behavior that would normally result in punishment or exile. But they did this within a religious context, serving as a mirror to show society its own contradictions and hypocrisies. They were holy fools, protected by their sacred status even as they disrupted the social order.

This was dangerous work. The sacred clown existed outside normal rules precisely because someone needed to occupy that space. They reminded the community that chaos always lurked at the edges of order, that the rules that governed daily life were arbitrary constructs that could be violated. They were necessary precisely because they were unsettling.

European traditions developed parallel figures. The court jester enjoyed protected status that allowed him to mock even the king. This wasn't mere entertainment. It was a pressure release valve for a rigidly hierarchical society. The jester could say what everyone thought but no one dared voice. He could point out the emperor's new clothes. He could tell truth to power because he occupied a liminal space where normal consequences didn't apply.

But this protection had limits. A jester who went too far could lose his head as quickly as any other courtier. The fool's bells and motley costume marked him as separate from normal society, but they also marked him as vulnerable. He was useful precisely because he was expendable. The king could laugh at mockery from a fool that he would execute if it came from a noble. The jester's low status paradoxically gave him freedom, but it was always freedom on a leash.

The Harlequin and Pierrot of the Commedia dell'arte tradition added another layer to the clown's evolution. These stock characters, originating in 16th century Italy, became archetypes that spread throughout European theater. Harlequin was the trickster servant, clever and acrobatic, wearing his distinctive diamond-patterned costume. Pierrot was the sad clown, the lovesick fool dressed in white with a tear painted on his cheek.

These figures were entertaining, yes, but they carried undertones of melancholy and danger. Harlequin's tricks often had a cruel edge. Pierrot's sadness suggested depths of suffering beneath the performance. They represented aspects of the human experience that couldn't be expressed directly in the rigid social contexts of their time. The mask and costume allowed performers to explore emotions and behaviors that would be unacceptable in everyday life.

Notice a pattern emerging? Throughout history, clowns have existed at boundaries. Sacred and profane. Order and chaos. Laughter and tears. Truth and deception. They've always occupied liminal spaces where normal rules don't apply. They've always been dangerous precisely because they operate outside the structures that govern everyone else.

The modern circus clown, the figure most people think of when they hear the word "clown," emerged in the late 18th and early 19th centuries. Joseph Grimaldi, performing in London in the early 1800s, essentially created the template for the modern clown. He developed the white face makeup, the exaggerated features, the physical comedy that would define clowning for the next two centuries.

Grimaldi's innovation was to take the theatrical traditions of Harlequin and Pierrot and transform them into something more extreme, more visceral, more focused on pure physical spectacle. His clown wasn't subtle. The makeup was stark white with bold red and black accents. The expressions were grotesque exaggerations. The comedy was violent, chaotic, built around pratfalls and slapstick that often resulted in actual injury.

Audiences loved it. Grimaldi became one of the most famous performers of his era, drawing massive crowds who came to watch him get hit, fall down, cause mayhem, and somehow survive it all with that painted grin still fixed on his face. But Grimaldi's personal life told a different story. He suffered from chronic pain due to the physical demands of his act. He struggled with alcoholism. His son, who followed him into clowning, died young from the same destructive patterns. Grimaldi himself died in poverty, his body broken by years of throwing himself down stairs and into walls for the entertainment of crowds.

The clown who makes others laugh while suffering in silence: this became another archetypal element of clown mythology. The idea that genuine misery hides behind the painted smile added a layer of tragedy to the figure. It suggested that the performance required a sacrifice, that becoming a clown meant surrendering your authentic self to the demands of the role.

By the mid-19th century, the circus had become the primary home for clowns. The traveling circus brought clowns to communities across America and Europe, making them a familiar part of popular culture. But the circus itself was a strange, liminal space. It appeared overnight in fields outside of town, a temporary city of tents and wagons. It brought exotic animals, death-defying acrobats, and yes, clowns. Then it vanished just as suddenly, leaving only trampled grass and fading memories.

The circus existed outside normal society, following its own rules, creating its own culture. Circus performers were often outcasts, people who didn't fit into conventional life. The circus became home to those who were too tall, too short, too strange for the regular world. Clowns fit perfectly into this context. They were already figures of boundary transgression, already operating outside normal social rules. The circus simply gave them a space where their strangeness was an asset rather than a liability.

This is when clowns became associated with children's entertainment, a connection that now seems inevitable but was actually quite recent. As circuses marketed themselves as family entertainment, clowns were positioned as figures that would particularly delight children. The logic seemed sound: children laugh easily, enjoy physical comedy, and haven't yet developed the social constraints that make adults uncomfortable with boundary violation.

But this created a fundamental tension that still exists today. Children were supposed to love clowns, but many children were (and are) terrified of them. Parents would bring their kids to the circus or hire clowns for birthday parties, expecting delight, and instead witness fear. The child would cry, try to hide, refuse to go near the painted figure. And the adults would say the child was being silly, that clowns were fun, that there was nothing to be afraid of.

Except the children were right. Their instincts, not yet overridden by social conditioning, correctly identified the clown as something wrong. The painted face that didn't match the voice. The smile that never changed. The unpredictable movements and boundary violations. These are all signals that humans are hardwired to recognize as threatening. Children saw what adults had trained themselves to ignore.

By the early 20th century, clowns had become culturally ubiquitous. They appeared in circuses, on stage, in early films. The great silent film comedians (Chaplin, Keaton, Lloyd) drew heavily on clown traditions in their work. Chaplin's Little Tramp was essentially a clown character, with his distinctive costume, his physical comedy, his ability to shift between humor and pathos. These performers brought clowning to a mass audience, cementing its place in popular culture.

But something else was happening simultaneously. Horror was discovering the clown. Early horror films and literature began using clown imagery to create unease. The German Expressionist film "The Man Who Laughs" (1928) featured a protagonist whose face was surgically mutilated into a permanent grin, creating an image that was simultaneously clownish and nightmarish. The fixed smile, unable to express any emotion except false joy, became a symbol of horror.

This dual nature (entertainment and terror existing in the same figure) intensified throughout the 20th century. Children's birthday parties featured clowns while horror stories used them as monsters. Circuses presented them as wholesome fun while artistic movements explored their darker implications. The clown became a Rorschach test, revealing more about the observer than the observed.

The 1970s and 1980s marked a turning point. This is when the cultural perception of clowns shifted decisively toward horror. John Wayne Gacy's arrest in 1978 revealed that a respected community member who performed as Pogo the Clown had murdered at least 33 young men. Stephen King's "It" (1986) gave us Pennywise, who became the definitive killer clown for a generation. The Joker evolved from campy Batman villain to genuinely frightening psychopath.

These weren't coincidences. They reflected a growing cultural awareness that the clown's traditional role (boundary transgressor, chaos agent, figure outside normal rules) made it a perfect vehicle for horror. The same qualities that supposedly made clowns entertaining also made them terrifying. The painted smile could hide anything. The costume could disguise any intent. The performance could mask any depravity.

Today, clowns exist primarily as figures of horror. Traditional circus clowns are increasingly rare as circuses themselves decline. Birthday party clowns are becoming obsolete, replaced by other forms of entertainment. But killer clowns are everywhere in horror media, from films to television to video games to internet creepypasta. The cultural transformation is complete. The clown has become what it perhaps always was: a figure of fear wearing the mask of joy.

The painted smile persists because it represents something fundamental about deception, about the gap between appearance and reality, about the monsters that hide behind friendly faces. We created clowns to make us laugh. Instead, we created the perfect symbol for everything we fear about trust, authenticity, and the darkness that lurks behind the performance we call civilization.

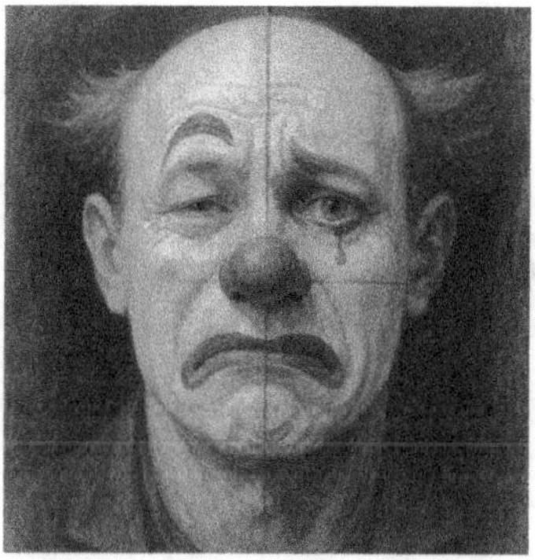

Chapter Two

The Psychology of the Creepy Clown

Why do clowns unsettle us? The question seems simple, but the answer reaches deep into human psychology, evolutionary biology, and the fundamental ways we process faces and social cues. The fear of clowns is not irrational, despite what we've been told. It's a perfectly logical response to a figure that violates almost every rule our brains use to assess safety and trustworthiness.

Let's start with the most basic element: the face. Human beings are extraordinarily good at reading faces. We can detect microexpressions that last less than a second. We can distinguish genuine smiles from fake ones by observing whether the muscles around the eyes engage. We can read emotion, intent, and trustworthiness from subtle shifts in facial expression that we're not even consciously aware of processing. This ability is not learned; it's hardwired into our brains from birth.

Infants only hours old already show preference for face-like patterns over other visual stimuli.

This expertise makes evolutionary sense. Humans survived as social animals by cooperating, and cooperation requires the ability to assess others quickly and accurately. Is this person friend or foe? Are they telling the truth or lying? Can I trust them with my children, my food, my safety? These questions could mean the difference between survival and death. We evolved sophisticated neural machinery dedicated entirely to processing faces and social cues.

A clown destroys all of this machinery.

The white greasepaint obliterates the natural variations in skin tone that our brains use to read blood flow and emotional state. When someone is embarrassed, angry, or lying, subtle changes in blood flow create barely perceptible color shifts in the face. We detect these unconsciously and use them to assess emotional state. White makeup erases these signals completely. The face becomes a blank canvas that provides no useful information.

On this blank canvas, new features are painted in grotesque exaggeration. The mouth is drawn far larger than any human mouth, often extending almost to the ears. This triggers what psychologists call the uncanny valley effect. The uncanny valley is the hypothesis that humanoid objects that imperfectly resemble actual human beings provoke eeriness and revulsion. The concept was first proposed by robotics professor Masahiro Mori in 1970, but it applies perfectly to clowns.

Here's how it works: We're comfortable with things that are clearly human and comfortable with things that are clearly not human. But things that fall in between (almost human but not quite) trigger deep discomfort. A cartoon is fine. A photograph of a person is fine. But a highly realistic robot or a person in heavy prosthetics falls into the uncanny valley, and our brains recoil.

Clowns live in the uncanny valley. They're clearly human (they move like humans, speak like humans), but their faces are wrong. The proportions are distorted. The colors are unnatural. The expressions don't change the way human expressions change. Our brains recognize this as human but not human, triggering an alarm response that something is fundamentally wrong.

The exaggerated features create additional problems. The enormous mouth, stretched into that permanent grin, shows too many teeth. In primates (including humans), bared teeth can signal either friendliness or aggression. We determine which based on context and the rest of the facial expression. But a clown's smile is frozen, unchanging, providing no context. Is this a friendly greeting or a threat display? Our brains cannot tell, so they assume the worst.

The eyes present an even bigger problem. Eyes are often called the windows to the soul for good reason. We read enormous amounts of information from eyes: where someone is looking, what they're focused on, their emotional state, their level of attention. The whites of human eyes (sclera) are larger and more visible than in other primates, specifically to facilitate this communication. Eye contact is one of the most important elements of human social interaction.

Clown makeup destroys this communication channel. Heavy black or colored rings around the eyes make them appear sunken, hollow, or dead. The exaggerated eyebrows (often painted far above where natural eyebrows would be) disconnect the eyes from the rest of the face, making expressions impossible to read. Some clowns paint tears below the eyes, adding a layer of contradiction: is the clown happy (that smile) or sad (those tears)? The mixed signals create confusion and unease.

This facial distortion has real psychological effects. Studies have shown that people have difficulty recognizing emotions in heavily made-up faces. The brain's fusiform face area (the region responsible for face recognition and processing) shows reduced activation when viewing clown faces compared to normal faces. Essentially, our brains struggle to process clowns as human faces at all. They register as something else, something wrong, something threatening.

Beyond the face, the clown's entire construction violates human norms. The wig (often in bright, unnatural colors) conceals the natural hair that we use to assess age, health, and identity. The costume obscures body shape, making it impossible to judge size, strength, or gender. Oversized shoes alter the gait, making movement unpredictable. Baggy clothing hides what the body is actually doing, preventing us from reading body language.

All of these elements combine to create a figure that our brains cannot properly process. We cannot read their emotions. We cannot predict their behavior. We cannot assess their intentions. Every system we have for evaluating safety and trustworthiness fails when confronted with a clown. And when those systems fail, our brains default to caution. They trigger the fight or flight response. They prepare us for danger.

This is not a bug in human psychology. It's a feature. Our ancestors who were too trusting, who ignored warning signs, who failed to recognize threats, did not survive to pass on their genes. We are descended from the cautious ones, the suspicious ones, the ones who erred on the side of assuming danger rather than safety. When we cannot read someone's face or predict their behavior, our instinct is to assume threat until proven otherwise.

Clowns have never been proven otherwise. They remain fundamentally unreadable, their painted faces offering no genuine information, their exaggerated features triggering every alarm our evolutionary history has installed in our brains.

The unpredictability of clown behavior compounds the visual unease. Clowns violate social norms as part of their performance. They invade personal space, touch strangers without permission, make loud unexpected noises, and engage in behavior that would be considered inappropriate or threatening in any other context. This violation of social rules is supposed to be funny, but it triggers deep psychological discomfort.

Human societies function through shared expectations about behavior. We have unspoken rules about how close to stand to strangers, when touching is appropriate, what volume is acceptable in different contexts. These rules vary by culture, but every culture has them. They create predictability, allowing us to navigate social situations without constant fear or confusion. When someone violates these rules, we instinctively recognize them as either ignorant of social norms (possibly dangerous due to lack of socialization) or deliberately transgressing them (definitely dangerous).

Clowns transgress deliberately. They get in your face. They honk horns next to your ear. They grab your hand or pat your head without asking. They create chaos where order should exist. This is their function, their entire purpose. But our psychological response to this behavior doesn't change just because we intellectually understand it's supposed to be entertainment. The instinctive reaction remains: this person does not follow rules, cannot be predicted, and therefore cannot be trusted.

Children respond to this more honestly than adults. A child who cries when a clown approaches is not being irrational. They're responding appropriately to a figure that violates every social rule they've been taught. Adults have learned to override this response, to tell themselves that clowns are harmless fun. But the underlying discomfort remains, waiting for the right trigger to surface.

The mask effect adds another layer of psychological complexity. Humans have a deep, ancient relationship with masks. Every culture in human history has used them for ritual, theater, or disguise. Masks allow the wearer to become someone or something else, to shed their normal identity and take on a new one. This transformation has always been viewed with a mixture of fascination and fear.

Psychologists have documented what they call deindividuation: the loss of self-awareness and individual accountability that occurs when someone's identity is concealed. Studies show that people behave more aggressively, more impulsively, and with less regard for consequences when wearing masks. The mask provides psychological distance from their actions, making it easier to do things they would never do with their face exposed.

Clown makeup functions as a mask, even though it's painted directly on the skin. It conceals identity just as effectively as a physical mask would. You cannot recognize someone in full clown makeup. You cannot read their true emotions. The person underneath becomes irrelevant; only the clown persona exists. This is psychologically liberating for the wearer and psychologically terrifying for everyone else.

What is the clown capable of doing behind that mask? Anything. There's no accountability, no identity to trace back to, no authentic person to hold responsible. The clown can do whatever it wants, and the person underneath can later claim it wasn't them, it was the character, the performance, the role. This separation between performer and performance creates a moral vacuum where normal rules and consequences don't apply.

The element of control (or lack thereof) is crucial to understanding clown fear. When you encounter a clown, you lose control of the interaction. The clown decides when to approach you, what to do, how to interact. You cannot predict their next move. You cannot enforce normal social boundaries because boundary violation is literally their job. You cannot even trust your own perceptual systems because the clown's appearance provides contradictory information that your brain cannot resolve.

This loss of control triggers anxiety in most people. We like to feel that we have some agency in our interactions, that we can withdraw if uncomfortable, that we can read situations and respond appropriately. Clowns strip away this agency. They make you part of their act whether you want to be or not. They can single you out of a crowd, force you into participation, make you the object of attention and laughter. And you cannot stop them without appearing rude, uptight, or afraid.

The laughter element deserves special attention. Laughter is a complex social signal with multiple meanings. It can indicate joy, but it can also indicate nervousness, discomfort, or even aggression. When a clown makes people laugh, what are they actually laughing at? Often, they're laughing at someone's discomfort or humiliation. The clown does something embarrassing or causes someone else to be embarrassed, and the crowd laughs.

This is not the laughter of shared joy. It's the laughter of relief (better them than me) or schadenfreude (pleasure at another's misfortune). Psychologically, this type of laughter reinforces social hierarchies and group cohesion by identifying an outsider who can be safely mocked. The clown facilitates this by being both the mocker and the mocked, the one who humiliates others while appearing ridiculous themselves.

But there's always an edge to this laughter, a sense that the joke could turn on you at any moment. You're laughing at the person the clown selected for their bit, but you could be next. This creates a state of anxious anticipation that's psychologically exhausting. You're never safe, never comfortable, always wondering when the clown's attention will fall on you.

Modern psychology has a term for the specific fear of clowns: coulrophobia. The term combines the Greek word for "stilt walker" (kolon) with phobia (fear). It's classified as a specific phobia, similar to fear of spiders or heights. But unlike most specific phobias, coulrophobia is not considered irrational by many psychologists who study it. The triggers for clown fear (unpredictability, inability to read emotions, violation of social norms, loss of control) are all legitimate reasons for caution.

Some researchers argue that coulrophobia isn't really a phobia at all, but a natural response to genuinely unsettling stimuli. The difference is important. A phobia is an irrational fear that interferes with daily life and should be treated through exposure therapy or other interventions. A natural, rational response to threatening stimuli should not be pathologized or "cured." It should be respected as a valid survival instinct.

The clown sits at the intersection of multiple psychological triggers: the uncanny valley, deindividuation, unpredictability, loss of control, and violation of social norms. It's not surprising that many people find them disturbing. What's surprising is that anyone finds them entertaining. Perhaps the entertainment value comes from the same place as horror entertainment: the thrill of controlled fear, of confronting something disturbing in a supposedly safe context.

But as we'll see in later chapters, that context isn't always as safe as we pretend.

Chapter Three

Coulrophobia: The Fear of Clowns

Coulrophobia is not a joke, despite how often it's treated as one. People who suffer from intense fear of clowns are frequently dismissed, mocked, or told to "get over it." The fear is presented as childish, irrational, something to be embarrassed about. But the reality is that coulrophobia is one of the most common specific fears, affecting a significant percentage of the population to varying degrees.

The exact prevalence is difficult to determine because many people who fear clowns never seek treatment or report their fear. They simply avoid situations where they might encounter clowns, which is relatively easy to do in modern life. Circuses are rare. Birthday party clowns are increasingly obsolete. Most people can go years without seeing a clown in person. But when confronted with one unexpectedly, the response can be severe: panic attacks, nausea, trembling, intense anxiety, and overwhelming urge to flee.

Unlike many phobias that develop from specific traumatic incidents, coulrophobia often exists without a clear origin point. People who fear clowns frequently cannot identify a specific event that triggered the fear. They simply remember always being afraid, or becoming afraid at a very young age without understanding why. This suggests that the fear may be partially innate rather than entirely learned.

Research into infant and child responses to clowns supports this theory. Studies have shown that children as young as four months old show distress responses to clown faces that they don't show to normal faces or even to other unusual stimuli. Their heart rates increase. They look away more frequently. They show signs of stress and discomfort. These children have had no negative experiences with clowns; they're responding to something fundamental about the clown's appearance that their developing brains recognize as wrong.

As children get older, the response often intensifies rather than diminishing. Toddlers and young children are at the peak age for coulrophobia. This is the age when they're developing sophisticated face recognition abilities, learning social norms, and becoming aware of danger. It's also the age when well-meaning parents are most likely to expose them to clowns at birthday parties, circuses, or other events.

The typical scenario plays out like this: A parent hires a clown for their child's birthday party, expecting delight. The clown arrives in full costume and makeup. The child takes one look at the painted face and begins screaming. The parent tries to calm the child, telling them the clown is nice, it's just pretend, there's nothing to be afraid of. The clown, trained to be persistent, tries to engage with the child anyway. The child's fear escalates to terror. Eventually, the clown gives up and entertains the other children while the frightened child hides, crying, until the clown leaves.

This experience can create or reinforce coulrophobia, but it's important to note that the fear existed before the event. The child wasn't afraid because the clown did something frightening. The child was afraid because the clown existed, because its appearance and behavior triggered deep psychological alarms that the child had no ability to override or rationalize.

Adults with coulrophobia describe similar visceral responses. They intellectually understand that most clowns are just performers trying to do their job. They know the fear is disproportionate to any actual threat. But knowledge doesn't diminish the fear. When confronted with a clown, the rational brain shuts down and the primitive survival instinct takes over. Fight or flight. Usually flight.

The physical symptoms of coulrophobia during an encounter with a clown can be severe. Rapid heartbeat, shortness of breath, dizziness, nausea, sweating, trembling, chest pain, and feelings of impending doom are all commonly reported. These are the same symptoms experienced during panic attacks, and they're triggered by the same neurological mechanisms: the amygdala (the brain's fear center) detecting a threat and flooding the body with stress hormones.

What's particularly interesting about coulrophobia is that it doesn't significantly diminish with exposure in the way many phobias do. Standard treatment for phobias involves gradual exposure to the feared stimulus in controlled conditions, allowing the patient to learn that the stimulus is not actually dangerous. But with clowns, exposure often reinforces rather than reduces the fear. People who are forced to interact with clowns don't typically become less afraid; they become more anxious about future encounters.

This suggests that the fear is based on something real rather than something imagined. When you expose someone with a spider phobia to harmless spiders repeatedly, they eventually learn that the spiders won't hurt them and the fear diminishes. But when you expose someone with clown fear to clowns, they don't learn that clowns are harmless. They learn that clowns continue to be unpredictable, to violate boundaries, to trigger discomfort. The exposure confirms rather than contradicts the original fear.

The cultural context of coulrophobia has shifted dramatically over the past few decades. In the mid-20th century, fear of clowns was considered unusual and irrational. Clowns were mainstream entertainment, featured prominently in circuses, children's television, and advertising. People who admitted to fearing clowns were viewed as oddities. But by the early 21st century, fear of clowns had become normalized and even expected. Clowns had migrated almost entirely into horror contexts, and admitting to finding them creepy was no longer unusual.

This cultural shift didn't create coulrophobia, but it validated it. People who had always felt uneasy around clowns but thought they were alone in this feeling discovered that millions of others shared the same response. Online communities formed where people could discuss their fear without judgment. The fear was given a name (coulrophobia), making it official and legitimate rather than merely personal and shameful.

Popular culture accelerated this validation. Every horror movie featuring a killer clown, every creepypasta about clowns in the woods, every Halloween costume depicting a terrifying clown reinforced the message that fear of clowns was not only acceptable but appropriate. The culture had caught up with what many people's instincts had been telling them all along: clowns are not to be trusted.

The psychological mechanisms underlying coulrophobia connect to several broader fear responses that humans have developed over millions of years of evolution. One of the most relevant is neophobia, the fear of anything new or unfamiliar. Young children are particularly prone to neophobia, which serves an important survival function. A toddler who approaches every unfamiliar creature or eats every unknown substance is unlikely to survive long. Caution around the unfamiliar is adaptive.

Clowns trigger neophobia because they are fundamentally unfamiliar. Yes, they're human underneath, but the costume and makeup transform them into something else, something that doesn't fit into any natural category. The child's brain asks: Is this a person? An animal? A monster? Unable to categorize the clown, the brain defaults to treating it as potentially dangerous until proven otherwise.

Another relevant mechanism is threat ambiguity. Humans are actually more frightened by ambiguous threats than by clear ones. If you see a lion charging at you, you're terrified but you know exactly what the threat is and how to respond (run, climb, fight if necessary). But if you hear something moving in the dark and can't identify what it is, the fear is often more intense because your imagination fills the gap with worst-case scenarios.

Clowns are maximally ambiguous. The painted face prevents you from reading emotions or intentions. The costume obscures the body. The behavior is unpredictable. You cannot determine what the clown wants, what it might do next, or whether it poses a threat. This ambiguity keeps the fear response activated continuously rather than allowing it to resolve into either safety (no threat detected) or clear danger (specific threat identified).

The concept of contamination also plays a role in coulrophobia. Humans have evolved strong disgust responses to things that might contaminate us with disease or decay. We're instinctively repelled by corpses, bodily fluids, rotting food, and other potential sources of contamination. Interestingly, clowns often trigger similar disgust responses despite not being obviously contaminated.

This may be because the heavy makeup and costume suggest concealment of the natural body, which our brains associate with hiding disease or deformity. The white face paint resembles the pallor of corpses. The exaggerated features suggest deformity or mutation. The bright, unnatural colors mimic the warning coloration of poisonous creatures. All of these elements trigger low-level disgust responses that compound the fear response.

Cultural transmission of fear also plays a significant role in coulrophobia. Children learn what to fear partly through direct experience but also through observing their parents' reactions. If a parent shows signs of fear or discomfort around clowns, children pick up on this and develop similar responses. In modern culture, where clowns are increasingly associated with horror rather than entertainment, children absorb these cultural messages even before encountering a real clown.

Media exposure is particularly powerful in transmitting clown fear. A child who has never seen a real clown but has encountered images of killer clowns in movies, television, or online content will approach their first real clown encounter with pre-existing fear. The real clown doesn't have to do anything threatening; the cultural association is already established. This creates a feedback loop where cultural representations of scary clowns make real clowns seem scary, which reinforces the cultural representation, which makes the next generation even more predisposed to fear.

Some psychologists argue that coulrophobia should not be classified as a true phobia at all because the fear response is proportionate to the actual ambiguity and unpredictability of the stimulus. A phobia, by definition, is an excessive or irrational fear. But if the clown genuinely does violate social norms, does obscure its true intentions, and does create legitimate uncertainty, then fearing it is not irrational. It's cautious.

This distinction has important implications for treatment. Traditional phobia treatment involves convincing the patient that their fear is disproportionate to the actual threat and helping them develop coping mechanisms to reduce anxiety. But if coulrophobia is actually a rational response to genuinely unsettling stimuli, then treatment should focus not on reducing the fear but on helping people avoid or manage encounters with clowns.

In practice, this is relatively easy. Adults with coulrophobia can simply choose not to attend circuses, avoid hiring clowns for parties, and walk away if they encounter a street performer in clown costume. Children with coulrophobia need their parents to respect their fear rather than forcing exposure in the belief that it will help them "get over it."

The intensity of coulrophobia varies widely among sufferers. Some people experience mild discomfort around clowns but can tolerate brief encounters. Others experience full panic attacks and cannot even look at images of clowns without severe anxiety. The severity often correlates with how unpredictable the encounter feels. A clown in a clearly defined performance context (on stage, at a distance, engaged with other people) is less threatening than a clown who approaches directly, invades personal space, and demands interaction.

Interestingly, coulrophobia does not typically extend to all masked or costumed figures. People who fear clowns don't necessarily fear mascots, theatrical performers in makeup, or people in Halloween costumes. The fear is specific to clowns, suggesting that it's the particular combination of elements (painted smile, exaggerated features, violation of social norms, unpredictable behavior) that triggers the response rather than costumes or masks in general.

Some sufferers report that certain types of clowns are more frightening than others. Traditional circus clowns with relatively subtle makeup and classic costumes are often less threatening than modern "horror clowns" with extreme makeup and deliberately frightening appearance. But even traditional clowns can trigger fear in people with severe coulrophobia. The fundamental elements (masked face, unpredictable behavior, boundary violation) are present regardless of how extreme the presentation is.

The persistence of coulrophobia into adulthood, despite social pressure to "grow out of it," demonstrates how deeply rooted the fear is. Adults with coulrophobia often report feeling embarrassed about their fear, knowing intellectually that it seems silly, but being unable to control their visceral response. This disconnect between intellectual understanding and emotional reaction is characteristic of fears based on deep evolutionary triggers rather than learned associations.

The brain's fear circuitry operates faster than its rational processing. When you encounter something your amygdala identifies as threatening, the fear response activates before your prefrontal cortex can analyze whether the threat is real. By the time you consciously think "it's just a performer in a costume," your body has already flooded with adrenaline and stress hormones. You can't think your way out of a response that happens before thought is possible.

This is why telling someone with coulrophobia to "just relax" or "realize it's not real" is useless. They already know it's not real in the sense of being a supernatural threat. But their brain recognizes it as real in the sense of being unpredictable, unreadable, and potentially dangerous. And in that sense, their brain is right.

Chapter Four

The Dark Side of Laughter: Clowns in Horror

Horror and comedy have always been closer than most people realize. Both genres rely on timing, misdirection, and subversion of expectations. Both build tension and release it suddenly. Both operate at the boundaries of social acceptability, exploring subjects that polite conversation avoids. The main difference is the emotional release: comedy aims for laughter, horror aims for screams. But the mechanisms are remarkably similar.

Clowns exist at the exact intersection of these two genres. They're supposed to be funny, but there's always been something unsettling lurking beneath the performance. The exaggerated movements, the painted face, the violation of social norms—these elements work equally well for comedy or horror depending on context and framing. Change the lighting, alter the music, shift the setting slightly, and the clown transforms from entertainer to nightmare.

Horror recognized this potential early. Even in the silent film era, filmmakers understood that clowns could be terrifying. "The Man Who Laughs" (1928), based on Victor Hugo's novel, featured Conrad Veidt as a man whose face had been mutilated into a permanent grin. Though not explicitly a clown, the character's fixed smile and tragic story created an image that influenced decades of horror iconography. The Joker's appearance would later be directly inspired by Veidt's performance, demonstrating how a smile divorced from joy becomes an image of horror.

The disconnect between appearance and reality is what makes clowns so effective in horror. A monster that looks like a monster is frightening, but predictable. We know what to expect. But a clown promises fun and delivers terror. It wears the costume of joy while embodying dread. This contradiction creates cognitive dissonance that amplifies the horror. Our expectations are violated at the most fundamental level.

Early horror literature explored this territory as well. Ray Bradbury's "Something Wicked This Way Comes" (1962) featured Mr. Dark's Pandemonium Shadow Show, a traveling carnival that brought supernatural evil to a small town. The carnival setting, with its clowns and performers, became a location of horror rather than entertainment. Bradbury understood that carnivals exist in liminal spaces, temporary towns that appear overnight and vanish just as quickly, leaving only memories and sometimes trauma.

The carnival or circus as horror setting became a recurring motif. These were places outside normal society, following their own rules, populated by people who didn't fit anywhere else. The freaks, the performers, the clowns—all existed at the margins. In horror fiction, these margins became gateways to something darker. The tent that looked cheerful from outside concealed horrors within. The clown that promised entertainment delivered nightmares.

But it was Stephen King's "It" (1986) that truly cemented the killer clown as a dominant horror archetype. Pennywise the Dancing Clown became the definitive image of clown horror for an entire generation. King took every unsettling element of clowns and amplified it, creating a monster that could appear as a clown precisely because clowns were already frightening. The novel worked because it articulated fears that readers had always felt but never fully understood.

King's genius was recognizing that he didn't need to make clowns scary. They already were. He just needed to make explicit what was always implicit. Pennywise's painted smile, his knowing eyes, his ability to appear where he shouldn't be, his promises of balloons and fun that masked murderous intent—all of these elements resonated because they tapped into existing unease about clowns. The novel validated coulrophobia, giving it form and name and cultural legitimacy.

The success of "It" opened floodgates. Horror creators realized that clowns were rich territory for terror. Films, books, comics, and television shows featuring killer clowns proliferated through the late 1980s and 1990s. Some were serious attempts at horror; others were cheap exploitation. But all of them contributed to a cultural shift where clowns became associated more with fear than with fun.

"Killer Klowns from Outer Space" (1988) took a different approach, blending horror with dark comedy. The film featured alien invaders who resembled circus clowns and used carnival weapons (cotton candy cocoons, popcorn guns, balloon animals that became real predators) to terrorize a town. The movie was absurd, campy, and shouldn't have worked. But it did, precisely because it recognized the inherent wrongness of clowns. The aliens didn't need to disguise themselves as something scary. Appearing as clowns was scary enough.

The film industry discovered that clown imagery was remarkably effective at generating dread with minimal effort. A figure in clown makeup standing in the wrong context (a dark alley, an empty parking lot, a child's bedroom at night) was immediately unsettling even before it did anything threatening. The costume did the work. Directors could create atmosphere and tension simply by placing a clown where it didn't belong.

This led to clowns becoming visual shorthand for horror. Music videos, album covers, haunted houses, and horror-themed attractions all began featuring clown imagery. The cultural association strengthened with each iteration. By the 2000s, an entire generation had grown up seeing clowns primarily in horror contexts. For them, clowns had never been fun. They had always been frightening.

The proliferation of clown horror created a feedback loop with real-world coulrophobia. People who might have been only mildly uncomfortable with clowns were exposed to increasingly extreme horror imagery, which reinforced and intensified their fear. Children who might have outgrown early clown anxiety instead had that anxiety validated and amplified by media. The cultural consensus shifted: clowns were no longer entertainers who some people found unsettling. They were horror figures that everyone recognized as frightening.

Horror video games discovered the potential of clowns as antagonists. The medium's interactivity made clown encounters particularly terrifying because players couldn't simply look away or fast-forward past the scary parts. They had to engage directly with the threat. Games like "Twisted Metal" featured Sweet Tooth, a killer clown driving an ice cream truck, hunting players through apocalyptic landscapes. The juxtaposition of childhood imagery (clowns, ice cream) with violence created deeply unsettling gameplay experiences.

Haunted attractions embraced clown horror with particular enthusiasm. Halloween haunts and horror-themed events discovered that actors in clown costumes generated strong reactions from visitors. The clowns could be aggressive, get in people's faces, violate personal space in ways that other characters couldn't. Visitors expected to be scared at a haunted house, but clowns scared them differently, more viscerally, triggering responses that went beyond enjoyable thrill into genuine distress.

This led to some haunted attractions creating entire clown-themed sections or even full clown-focused events. Visitors would navigate through areas filled with clowns in various states of decay, madness, or malevolence. These proved extremely popular with thrill-seekers while being absolutely unbearable for people with coulrophobia. The attractions had to start posting warnings: if you fear clowns, do not enter.

The internet age brought new dimensions to clown horror. Creepypasta stories (user-generated horror fiction shared online) frequently featured clowns. These stories spread rapidly through social media, reaching audiences who might never read a horror novel or watch a horror film. The low barrier to entry meant anyone could write and share a clown horror story, flooding the internet with thousands of variations on the killer clown theme.

Some of these stories were sophisticated and genuinely frightening. Others were crude and poorly written. But quantity had its own effect. The sheer volume of clown horror content online reinforced the cultural association between clowns and fear. Someone casually browsing the internet would encounter clown horror imagery and stories regularly, even if they weren't actively seeking horror content.

Internet memes took clown horror in unexpected directions. Images of clowns were edited, distorted, combined with disturbing text or other imagery, and shared as jokes that weren't entirely jokes. The humor was dark, uncomfortable, based on shared recognition that clowns were inherently creepy. These memes spread the association between clowns and horror to people who might never consume traditional horror media.

The visual language of horror clowns evolved and standardized during this period. Certain elements became clichés: the cracked or smeared makeup suggesting decay or madness, the too-wide grin revealing damaged or pointed teeth, the dead or glowing eyes, the addition of blood (often inexplicably present on the costume), the positioning of the clown in liminal spaces like empty hallways or dark woods. These visual markers became instantly recognizable signals that this was a horror clown, not an entertainment clown.

Television embraced clown horror as well. "American Horror Story: Freak Show" (2014) featured Twisty the Clown, a disfigured performer who kidnapped and murdered people while wearing a grotesque homemade mask. The character's backstory was tragic (he was a genuine entertainer driven to madness by cruelty and misunderstanding), but his appearance and actions were pure nightmare fuel. Twisty became one of the most memorable characters in the series despite appearing in only a handful of episodes.

The show's creators understood that clowns required minimal explanation in horror contexts. They didn't need to justify why Twisty was frightening. His appearance did that work instantly. The reveal of what lay beneath his mask (a mutilated face held together by the mask itself) was horrifying, but arguably no more horrifying than the mask itself. The clown costume was already a signifier of monstrosity.

Horror anthologies and short film collections began including clown-themed entries almost as a requirement. The format worked well for clown horror because the stories didn't need extensive setup.

A clown appears in the wrong place, at the wrong time, and horror unfolds. The efficiency of clown horror made it perfect for short-form content. A five-minute film could generate substantial dread simply by having a clown stand silently in an unexpected location.

The aesthetics of horror clowns influenced fashion, music, and art outside the horror genre. Musicians adopted clown makeup for stage personas, understanding that it projected danger and unpredictability. Visual artists incorporated clown imagery into work exploring themes of identity, deception, and societal collapse. Fashion designers created collections inspired by carnival and circus aesthetics but filtered through a horror lens, with distressed fabrics, unsettling proportions, and makeup that suggested decay rather than celebration.

This cultural diffusion meant that even people who actively avoided horror media encountered clown horror imagery regularly. It had escaped its genre boundaries and permeated broader culture. The clown was no longer just a horror villain; it had become a symbol, a visual language that communicated complex ideas about authenticity, performance, and hidden darkness.

Academic and critical analysis of clown horror emerged as the phenomenon became impossible to ignore. Scholars examined what clowns represented in contemporary horror: the failure of innocence, the corruption of childhood, the mask that modern society requires everyone to wear. The clown became a metaphor for late capitalism's demand that we perform happiness regardless of our actual emotional state, that we smile for the camera even when suffering, that we maintain the performance no matter the cost.

This metaphorical weight made clown horror resonate beyond simple scares. The killer clown wasn't just a monster; it was a critique. It exposed the violence inherent in forced cheerfulness, the danger of ignoring genuine emotion in favor of performed positivity, the cost of maintaining masks that don't reflect reality. When the clown's smile turned murderous, it was revealing the aggression that had always lurked beneath the performance of joy.

Horror creators recognized this depth and began crafting clown stories with more sophisticated themes. The clown became a vehicle for exploring trauma, discussing mental illness, examining social expectations, and questioning the nature of identity. These weren't just slasher films with clown antagonists; they were using the clown as a complex symbol to discuss genuine human concerns.

But beneath all the metaphor and meaning, one simple truth remained: clowns were effective in horror because they were already frightening. Everything else was elaboration on that fundamental fact. The painted smile, the hidden face, the unpredictable behavior—these elements had always contained horror potential. The genre simply recognized what children and people with coulrophobia had known all along.

The clown didn't need to become a monster. It already was one. Horror just stopped pretending otherwise.

Chapter Five

Killer Clowns in Pop Culture

The killer clown has become one of pop culture's most enduring and recognizable archetypes. From films to television, from video games to music, from internet memes to Halloween costumes, the image of the murderous clown saturates contemporary media. This ubiquity is remarkable considering that clowns were, for most of the 20th century, associated primarily with wholesome entertainment. The transformation from circus performer to cultural monster happened rapidly and completely.

The evolution can be traced through specific cultural moments and iconic characters that shaped public perception. Each major killer clown in popular media built on what came before, adding new elements while reinforcing the core concept: the clown that smiles while it kills, that promises fun while delivering death, that wears the mask of joy to conceal monstrosity.

One of the earliest and most influential film depictions came with the Italian giallo horror movement of the 1970s. These stylized thriller films often featured masked killers, and several incorporated clown imagery. The mask served a practical narrative purpose (concealing the killer's identity until the reveal) but also generated psychological unease. A killer in a ski mask is frightening but comprehensible. A killer in a clown mask is disturbing on a deeper level because it perverts symbols meant to represent innocence and joy.

The slasher film boom of the 1980s embraced this potential enthusiastically. While Jason Voorhees had his hockey mask and Michael Myers had his pale featureless mask, numerous lower-budget slashers experimented with clown killers. Many of these films were forgettable, but they contributed to a growing cultural database of clown horror imagery. Audiences became accustomed to seeing clowns as threats rather than entertainers.

"Poltergeist" (1982), while not primarily about clowns, featured a scene that traumatized an entire generation of viewers. A young boy's clown doll, sitting innocuously on a chair, comes to life and attacks him. The scene worked because it violated the expected safety of a child's bedroom and transformed a supposedly friendly object into an attacker. The clown doll became one of the film's most memorable elements despite minimal screen time, demonstrating the efficiency of clown imagery in generating fear.

That scene influenced countless subsequent horror films and television episodes. The evil clown doll or toy became a recurring motif. "Poltergeist" had proven that you didn't need a full-sized clown to create terror; even a representation of a clown, a toy version, could trigger deep unease. This expanded the range of horror storytelling, allowing clown fear to infiltrate domestic spaces through seemingly innocent objects.

The 1990s saw killer clowns transition from B-movie villains to more prominent cultural figures. The television miniseries adaptation of Stephen King's "It" (1990) brought Pennywise to millions of viewers, many of whom had never read the novel. Tim Curry's performance as the demonic clown created an iconic image that defined killer clowns for a generation. His Pennywise was seductive and terrifying, playful and murderous, capable of shifting from childlike innocence to predatory menace in seconds.

The miniseries had limitations due to television standards and special effects technology of the era, but Curry's performance transcended these constraints. His Pennywise understood something crucial: the horror wasn't in the monster's true form (the spider-like entity beneath the clown appearance) but in the clown mask itself. The most frightening moments came not when Pennywise transformed into something else, but when he remained a clown while doing terrible things.

This realization influenced subsequent depictions of killer clowns. The most effective ones didn't abandon the clown appearance to reveal a "true" monster underneath. They remained clowns throughout, proving that the clown itself was monster enough. The painted smile while committing murder was more disturbing than any fangs or claws could be.

Music embraced killer clown imagery during this period as well. The horrorcore hip-hop movement, exemplified by groups like Insane Clown Posse, adopted clown personas and violent imagery. Their music videos, album covers, and stage performances featured clown makeup combined with dark, aggressive themes. While not horror in the traditional sense, they contributed to the cultural association between clowns and danger, violence, and transgression.

Heavy metal and industrial music also incorporated clown imagery. Band members adopted clown makeup for performances, understanding that it projected menace and unpredictability. The clown face became a rebellion against expectations, a way of signaling that the performance would violate norms and comfort zones. It was armor and weapon simultaneously, protecting the performer's identity while projecting threat.

The late 1990s and early 2000s saw a proliferation of killer clown films of varying quality. Some were genuine attempts at psychological horror, others were slasher films with clown aesthetics, and many were low-budget direct-to-video productions capitalizing on the popularity of the archetype. Quality varied wildly, but the sheer volume reinforced the cultural saturation of killer clown imagery.

"Spawn" (1997) featured a violent villain called Violator who could take the form of a grotesque clown. The character was simultaneously comedic and threatening, using crude humor while committing brutal violence. This combination of comedy and horror in a single clown character demonstrated the genre's flexibility. The clown could be funny and terrifying in the same moment, the laughter and the screams existing simultaneously.

Video games discovered that clowns made excellent antagonists because their unpredictability translated well to gameplay mechanics. Players couldn't anticipate what a clown enemy would do next, creating genuine tension during encounters. The "Batman: Arkham" series featured the Joker prominently, and while we'll discuss him in depth in a later chapter, his presence in these games demonstrated how clown aesthetics could enhance interactive horror experiences.

Indie horror games took this further. Titles like "Five Nights at Freddy's" and similar games featured animatronic entertainers (including clown-like characters) that hunted the player through confined spaces. The games tapped into childhood fears of mascots and performers, using jump scares and atmospheric dread to create intensely uncomfortable experiences. The success of these games proved that clown horror resonated strongly with younger audiences who had grown up seeing clowns primarily in horror contexts.

The internet age transformed killer clown culture in fundamental ways. Creepypasta stories spread rapidly, with clown-themed tales among the most popular. "Laughing Jack," a creepypasta about an imaginary friend who transforms into a killer clown, became one of the most widely shared horror stories online. The character spawned countless fan artworks, derivative stories, and even cosplay, demonstrating how internet culture could amplify and evolve killer clown mythology.

Social media platforms became vehicles for spreading clown horror imagery. Users shared photoshopped images of clowns in unsettling contexts, created and distributed short horror videos featuring clowns, and developed elaborate fictional narratives about clown sightings and attacks. Some of this content was clearly labeled as fiction; much of it blurred the line between story and reality, creating ambiguity that enhanced the horror.

This culminated in the 2016 clown sighting phenomenon, which we'll examine in detail in the next chapter. But the groundwork for that cultural moment was laid by decades of clown horror saturation in pop culture. When people began reporting real clowns in threatening contexts, the public reaction was shaped by years of consuming media that presented clowns as dangerous. The cultural narrative was already established; reality simply seemed to confirm it.

Streaming services and premium cable networks contributed to killer clown proliferation as well. With fewer content restrictions than broadcast television, shows could present more extreme and disturbing clown imagery. "American Horror Story" devoted significant attention to Twisty the Clown, creating a character whose appearance was so disturbing that promotional images alone generated complaints. The show's creators later toned down Twisty's design for future appearances because the original was deemed too extreme even for horror fans.

The 2017 film adaptation of "It" brought Pennywise back to cultural prominence with a new interpretation by Bill Skarsgård. This version was more overtly monstrous than Tim Curry's portrayal, with inhuman features and movements that emphasized the creature's alien nature. The film became a massive commercial success, demonstrating that killer clown horror had broad mainstream appeal beyond genre audiences.

The success of "It" sparked renewed interest in killer clown content across all media. Studios greenlit clown-themed horror projects. Publishers sought manuscripts featuring killer clowns. Independent creators produced clown horror content for YouTube and other platforms. The cultural appetite for killer clowns seemed insatiable, with each new iteration finding an audience eager for more variations on the theme.

Halloween costume sales reflected this cultural shift. Killer clown costumes became perennial best-sellers, outselling traditional monster costumes like vampires and werewolves. The costumes ranged from relatively tame interpretations to extremely graphic and disturbing designs. Some retailers faced criticism for selling costumes deemed too frightening, particularly in light of the 2016 clown sightings which had caused genuine public fear.

The commercialization of killer clown imagery created an interesting paradox. Clowns were genuinely frightening to many people, triggering real anxiety and fear. Yet this fear was being marketed and sold as entertainment. People who would never attend a circus bought tickets to see horror films about killer clowns. Individuals with coulrophobia avoided real clowns but consumed media depicting clowns as monsters. The cultural relationship with clowns had become complex and contradictory.

Fashion and visual culture absorbed killer clown aesthetics as well. High fashion photo shoots incorporated clown makeup and circus themes filtered through a dark, unsettling lens. Street artists created murals featuring menacing clowns. Graphic designers used clown imagery to convey danger, chaos, and subversion. The killer clown had transcended its origins in horror genre to become a broader cultural symbol.

Music videos across genres incorporated killer clown imagery. Pop artists used it for shock value and edge. Rock and metal bands used it to project danger and rebellion. Even country and folk musicians occasionally employed clown imagery in videos exploring darker themes. The versatility of the killer clown symbol allowed it to function across widely different musical contexts and audiences.

Comic books and graphic novels explored killer clown themes extensively. Beyond the Joker, numerous other clown villains populated superhero comics. Horror comics featured clowns as both protagonists and antagonists. The visual medium of comics was particularly suited to depicting the striking imagery of killer clowns, allowing artists to create memorable and disturbing designs that lingered in readers' minds.

The proliferation reached a saturation point where nearly everyone in Western culture had been exposed to killer clown imagery regardless of their interest in horror. You couldn't avoid it. Television commercials, billboard advertisements, news coverage of the clown sightings, casual references in sitcoms and dramas all reinforced the association between clowns and fear. The cultural consensus was complete: clowns were no longer entertainers. They were monsters.

This total transformation happened in roughly four decades, from the late 1970s to the present. A figure that had been culturally associated with children's entertainment and circuses for over a century was completely reimagined as a source of terror. The speed and completeness of this shift is remarkable and suggests that the killer clown imagery tapped into something authentic and powerful in the collective psyche.

Pop culture didn't create the fear of clowns. The fear was already there, waiting to be acknowledged and expressed. Pop culture simply gave it permission, validation, and endless variations. The killer clown became a mirror reflecting our anxieties about trust, authenticity, and the masks we all wear. And unlike the painted smile on the clown's face, this reflection showed something true.

Chapter Six

The 2016 Clown Sightings: Mass Hysteria or Social Experiment?

In August 2016, something strange began happening in Greenville, South Carolina. Residents reported seeing people dressed as clowns attempting to lure children into the woods near an apartment complex. The clowns were described as standing at the edge of tree-lines, waving at children, offering money or candy. Police investigated but found no evidence of actual clowns. No arrests were made. No clowns were located.

This should have been the end of it. A few isolated reports, likely misidentifications or children's imaginations, investigated and dismissed. Instead, it was the beginning of a phenomenon that would spread across the United States and eventually worldwide, creating genuine panic and revealing something disturbing about our cultural relationship with clowns.

Within weeks, similar reports emerged from other parts of South Carolina, then neighboring states, then across the country. People dressed as clowns were reportedly appearing in unexpected places: woods, parking lots, street corners at night, outside schools, near playgrounds. Sometimes they just stood and watched. Sometimes they followed people. Sometimes they carried weapons or objects that might be weapons. Sometimes they chased people. Sometimes they tried to lure children.

The reports varied wildly in credibility. Some came with photographic or video evidence, though much of it was blurry, distant, or obviously staged. Some were clearly hoaxes or attempts at viral fame. Some were likely misidentifications of legitimate clown performers or people in costume for unrelated reasons. But some reports seemed genuine, coming from multiple witnesses, corroborated by physical evidence, reported to police with obvious sincerity and fear.

Law enforcement agencies were overwhelmed. Police departments across the country received thousands of clown-related calls in the span of a few months. Some departments issued official statements urging calm. Others took the reports seriously, increasing patrols and warning residents to be vigilant. A few arrested people for clown-related offenses, charging them with making terroristic threats, disorderly conduct, or inducing panic.

Schools went into lockdown. Districts sent letters home to parents assuring them of increased security. Some schools banned clown costumes entirely, even for Halloween, to prevent panic. Teachers reported that students were genuinely frightened, that the atmosphere in schools had changed, that children who normally walked home were now afraid to do so.

Social media amplified the phenomenon exponentially. Reports of clown sightings spread instantly across Facebook, Twitter, and Instagram. Hashtags like #ClownSightings and #CreepyClown trended nationally and then globally. People shared blurry photos, unverified videos, and secondhand accounts. The signal-to-noise ratio became impossible to determine. Real sightings (if they existed) were buried under mountains of hoaxes, jokes, and attempts at viral fame.

The media coverage was intense and often irresponsible. News outlets ran stories about clown sightings with minimal verification, often presenting unconfirmed social media reports as fact. The coverage itself became a story, with meta-analysis of why people were so afraid of clowns and whether the fear was justified. Psychologists were interviewed. Coulrophobia was discussed on national news. The cultural conversation became recursive, feeding on itself.

This media attention created a self-fulfilling prophecy. People who might have ignored a person in a clown costume before August 2016 now saw them as potential threats. Legitimate clown performers (the few who still existed) found themselves subjected to suspicion and hostility. Some reported being threatened or attacked simply for wearing their professional costume in public. The cultural consensus had shifted: clowns in public spaces were now presumed dangerous until proven otherwise.

Professional clowns' organizations issued statements condemning the sightings and the people responsible for them. They emphasized that real clowns were entertainers, not threats, and that the clown sightings were damaging their profession and livelihood. But these statements had little impact. The public didn't distinguish between "real" clowns and the people dressing as clowns to frighten others. The costume itself had become the threat, regardless of who wore it or why.

The phenomenon spread internationally. Reports of clown sightings emerged from the United Kingdom, Australia, Canada, and other countries. The specific details varied by location and culture, but the core pattern remained: people in clown costumes appearing in unexpected places, generating fear and sometimes panic. The internet had globalized what might once have remained a localized oddity.

Theories about the sightings proliferated. Some suggested it was a coordinated marketing campaign for a horror film or television show. Several entertainment properties were suspected, though all denied involvement. Some theorized it was a social experiment examining mass hysteria and social media amplification. Others suggested it was simply copycat behavior, with each report inspiring new people to don clown costumes and frighten others for attention or amusement.

The truth was likely a combination of all these factors plus others harder to categorize. Some sightings were probably hoaxes from the start. Some were legitimate performers caught in the wrong place at the wrong time. Some were pranks that escalated beyond the prankster's intentions. Some were deliberate attempts to frighten people. And some may never have happened at all, existing only as social media posts and rumors that took on the appearance of reality through repetition.

What made the 2016 clown sightings particularly interesting from a psychological and cultural perspective was the intensity of the public response. People weren't just mildly concerned or amused. They were genuinely terrified. Communities organized armed patrols. Parents kept children home from school. Police departments devoted significant resources to investigating reports. The fear was real, visceral, and widespread.

This response revealed something crucial about our cultural relationship with clowns. When clowns appeared in unexpected contexts (not at circuses or parties but in woods and parking lots at night), the public didn't laugh. They didn't dismiss it as harmless pranks. They reacted as if under genuine threat, because on some fundamental level, the threat felt real.

The woods became a particularly significant location in the mythology of the sightings. Multiple reports described clowns standing at treelines, lurking between trees, or attempting to lure people into forested areas. This setting tapped into ancient fears about what waits in the wilderness beyond civilization's boundaries. The woods represent the unknown, the uncontrolled, the place where rules don't apply. A clown in the woods combined modern and primal fears into something uniquely disturbing.

Law enforcement's varied responses highlighted the ambiguity of the situation. Was this a real threat requiring serious investigation, or mass hysteria that needed to be calmly debunked? Different departments made different choices. Some treated every report as credible, deploying officers to investigate, increasing patrols, and making arrests when possible. Others issued statements urging the public not to panic, emphasizing that most reports were unsubstantiated and that clown costumes were not inherently illegal.

Several arrests were made during this period, though the charges varied. Some people were arrested for making terroristic threats after posting on social media about being "clowns" who would attack schools or harm children. Others were arrested for disorderly conduct or inducing panic after actually appearing in public in clown costumes and frightening people. A few were charged with more serious offenses when they carried weapons or actually attempted to harm someone.

These arrests raised legal and philosophical questions. Is wearing a clown costume in public a crime? If someone is genuinely frightened by a clown, is the person wearing the costume responsible for that fear?

Where is the line between harmless prank and criminal threat? The legal system struggled to apply existing laws to a situation they weren't designed to address.

Schools became flashpoints for clown-related panic. Threats were posted on social media warning that clowns would attack specific schools on specific dates. These threats were almost certainly hoaxes, but schools couldn't take that risk. Lockdowns were implemented. Police presence increased. Parents were notified. In some cases, schools closed entirely based on clown-related threats. The disruption to education was significant and widespread.

The threats targeting schools revealed the malicious potential of the clown sighting phenomenon. Whether or not the original sightings were genuine, they had created an environment where anonymous threats could generate real fear and real consequences. The clown had become a weapon, a way to disrupt communities and terrorize people without physical presence or actual violence.

Halloween 2016 became particularly fraught. Traditionally, clown costumes were popular Halloween choices. But in 2016, many retailers pulled clown costumes from shelves. Schools banned them explicitly. Communities issued warnings about clown costumes potentially triggering panic or even violence. Some individuals who had planned clown costumes chose alternatives to avoid being mistaken for the threatening clowns from the sightings.

Paradoxically, this also made clown costumes more popular among certain groups precisely because they were controversial and frightening. Teenage and young adult Halloween partygoers embraced killer clown costumes as edgy and provocative. The taboo enhanced the appeal. Wearing a clown costume in 2016 was a statement, a deliberate choice to embrace the fear and controversy.

The phenomenon began to fade in November 2016, declining as rapidly as it had emerged. Reports became less frequent. Media coverage decreased. The cultural moment passed. But it left lasting effects on how clowns were perceived and how communities responded to perceived threats amplified by social media.

Analysis of the phenomenon offered various explanations. From a psychological perspective, it demonstrated how fear can spread through social networks faster than reason or verification. Each report of a clown sighting primed people to see clowns everywhere, to interpret ambiguous stimuli as threats, to believe rumors because everyone else seemed to believe them. The phenomenon was a real-world demonstration of social contagion and collective anxiety.

From a cultural perspective, the sightings revealed that decades of killer clown imagery in pop culture had fundamentally altered how people perceived clowns. When faced with a clown in an unexpected context, people defaulted to assuming danger rather than entertainment. The cultural narrative (clowns are threats) had become so dominant that it overrode other possible interpretations.

The role of social media was crucial and disturbing. Platforms designed to connect people and share information became vectors for spreading fear. The viral nature of content meant that a single false report could reach millions within hours. The lack of verification mechanisms allowed hoaxes to circulate alongside genuine reports, making it impossible for users to distinguish truth from fiction. The algorithm-driven amplification meant that the most sensational and frightening content spread fastest.

Some commentators argued that the clown sightings were a preview of broader problems with social media and collective reality. If thousands of people could be convinced that clowns were lurking in woods across the country based on largely unverified reports and blurry photos, what else could they be convinced of? The phenomenon demonstrated how easily fear and misinformation could spread through digital networks, overwhelming truth and reason.

Others saw it as a form of collective play, a cultural ghost story that people participated in even while half-knowing it wasn't real. The ambiguity was part of the appeal. You couldn't be certain the clowns weren't real, so engaging with the phenomenon (sharing reports, being cautious, discussing it with friends) was a low-stakes way of participating in something exciting and scary.

The 2016 clown sightings proved that our fear of clowns is not abstract or theoretical. When confronted with the possibility of real clowns in threatening contexts, communities responded with genuine fear and took serious protective measures. The painted smile, when removed from controlled entertainment settings and placed in the wild, became a legitimate object of terror. The cultural transformation of the clown from entertainer to monster was complete. And unlike horror movies or Halloween attractions, this time the fear wasn't contained by fiction. It spilled into reality, if only for a few months, and showed us exactly how deeply the fear runs.

Chapter Seven

The Joker: The Ultimate Killer Clown

The Joker is not technically a clown. He has never performed in a circus, never entertained children at birthday parties, never belonged to the traditional world of clowning. Yet he is perhaps the most iconic and influential killer clown in popular culture. His painted face, his permanent grin, his chaotic violence, and his philosophical nihilism have defined what it means to be a terrifying clown for generations of audiences.

Created by Bill Finger, Bob Kane, and Jerry Robinson, the Joker first appeared in Batman comics in 1940. The character's visual design was inspired by Conrad Veidt's performance in "The Man Who Laughs," that silent film featuring a character with a face mutilated into a permanent grin. From the beginning, the Joker was associated with the horror of the fixed smile, the face that cannot stop grinning even when committing murder.

Early comic book versions of the Joker were relatively straightforward villains. He committed crimes, fought Batman, and usually ended up captured or apparently killed, only to return in future issues. The clown aesthetic was present but not particularly emphasized. He was a criminal who happened to have clown-like appearance and tendencies toward theatrical crimes. The deeper psychological horror of the character hadn't yet been fully developed.

The character evolved significantly over decades of comic book history. Different writers and artists brought different interpretations, but certain core elements remained constant: the white face, the green hair, the red lips stretched into that grin, and the purple suit. These visual markers became so iconic that the Joker could be recognized instantly even in silhouette. The aesthetic had achieved archetypal status.

The 1989 film "Batman," directed by Tim Burton and featuring Jack Nicholson as the Joker, brought the character to massive mainstream audiences. Nicholson's performance emphasized the character's showmanship and dark humor while adding genuinely disturbing elements. His Joker was funny and terrifying simultaneously, capable of dancing to Prince music while gassing people to death, of making jokes while committing atrocities.

Burton's film established the origin story that would influence most subsequent versions: a criminal falls into a vat of chemicals during a confrontation with Batman, emerging with his face permanently bleached white and his mind shattered. The accident transforms him into the Joker, creating the painted face that cannot be removed, the smile that cannot be erased, the performance that cannot end. The tragedy is that the mask has become permanent, fused to the flesh, making the clown persona inescapable.

This origin story resonates because it literalizes what all clowns represent metaphorically: the person trapped behind the performance, unable to remove the mask, forced to smile regardless of what they actually feel. The Joker's condition is the clown's condition taken to its logical extreme. He cannot stop being the Joker. The painted face is his real face now.

Nicholson's Joker was charismatic and entertaining, a villain audiences could enjoy watching even while recognizing his evil. This set a template for future interpretations: the Joker should be fun to watch, but the fun should be disturbing, unsettling, tinged with genuine menace. The character walks a tightrope between comedy and horror, and the best interpretations maintain that balance without falling entirely into either category.

The animated series "Batman: The Animated Series" (1992-1995) featured a Joker voiced by Mark Hamill that became definitive for many fans. This version emphasized the character's unpredictability and capacity for sudden violence. Hamill's vocal performance could shift from playful to psychotic in an instant, creating a Joker who was genuinely frightening despite being in a children's cartoon. The animated format allowed for exaggerated expressions and movements that enhanced the clown-like qualities while the writing and voice acting provided depth and menace.

This Joker demonstrated that the character didn't need to be realistic or grounded to be effective. The heightened, almost theatrical presentation worked because it was true to the clown archetype. Clowns are supposed to be exaggerated, oversized, more intense than real life. Making the Joker cartoonish didn't diminish his threat; it enhanced it by making him more alien, more unpredictable, more fundamentally wrong.

Heath Ledger's portrayal in "The Dark Knight" (2008) revolutionized how audiences and creators thought about the Joker. This version abandoned the origin story entirely. The Joker tells multiple contradictory stories about his scars, implying that the truth doesn't matter, that he's created himself through performance and will. His makeup is smeared and imperfect, suggesting he applies it himself rather than it being permanent. He's less polished than previous versions, more genuinely disturbing, operating from motivations that seem barely comprehensible.

Ledger's Joker was a force of pure chaos, a philosophical argument against order and meaning wrapped in clown makeup. His famous monologues about chaos and anarchy, his social experiments forcing people to choose between self-preservation and morality, his complete rejection of conventional goals like wealth or power—all of this elevated the character beyond typical villainy into something more disturbing and complex.

The performance was so intense and transformative that it became inseparable from Ledger's tragic death shortly after filming completed. The Joker seemed to have consumed the actor, blurring the line between performance and reality in ways that added another layer of darkness to the character. Whether or not the role actually contributed to Ledger's death (a claim disputed by those who knew him), the cultural perception linked them inextricably.

This version of the Joker proved that the character could carry serious thematic weight. He wasn't just a colorful villain for a superhero to fight. He represented genuine philosophical questions about human nature, social order, and whether civilization is merely a thin veneer over underlying chaos. The clown makeup became a visual representation of these ideas: the performance we all engage in, the masks we wear, the pretense that separates us from anarchy.

Ledger's Joker influenced countless subsequent portrayals in comics, films, television, and other media. The interpretation became so dominant that it overshadowed previous versions. Creators began emphasizing the character's chaos and nihilism over his clownishness, though the visual markers remained. The Joker became less about literally being a clown and more about what clowns represent symbolically: the destruction of meaning, the rejection of social norms, the embrace of chaos.

Jared Leto's brief appearance as the Joker in "Suicide Squad" (2016) attempted a different approach, presenting a more overtly criminal and sexualized version of the character. This Joker was a gangster who happened to have clown aesthetics rather than a clown who happened to be a criminal. The interpretation was controversial and generally considered less successful than Ledger's, demonstrating that not all approaches to the character resonate equally.

Todd Phillips' "Joker" (2019), starring Joaquin Phoenix, took yet another radical departure. This film presented an origin story grounded in social realism, portraying Arthur Fleck as a mentally ill man failed by society who gradually transforms into the Joker. Phoenix's performance emphasized the character's pain and isolation, making him simultaneously sympathetic and terrifying. His laugh—a medical condition causing him to laugh involuntarily at inappropriate times—becomes a horrifying inversion of what laughter is supposed to represent.

Phoenix's Joker is perhaps the most explicitly clown-focused version. Arthur works as a professional party clown before his transformation, and the film explores what it means to be forced to perform happiness while suffering internally. The painted smile becomes a form of rebellion, a way of embracing the performance so completely that it becomes authentic. If society demands that he smile, he'll smile—but the smile will mean something different, something dangerous.

The film sparked intense debate about whether it glorified violence or provided too sympathetic a portrayal of a mass murderer. These controversies demonstrated the Joker's cultural power. The character had transcended entertainment to become a symbol that different groups interpreted in radically different ways. Some saw a critique of how society treats the mentally ill and the marginalized. Others saw dangerous valorization of violent nihilism.

This interpretive flexibility is part of what makes the Joker the ultimate killer clown. The character can be reimagined endlessly while retaining core elements that make him recognizable. The painted face, the smile, the chaos, the rejection of meaning—these elements can be emphasized or downplayed, combined with different themes and settings, but they persist across all versions.

The Joker's relationship with Batman is crucial to understanding the character's resonance. Batman represents order, control, the belief that trauma can be channeled into purpose. The Joker represents chaos, abandon, the belief that trauma destroys meaning rather than creating it. They're mirror images, two responses to a world that doesn't make sense. The Joker is what Batman could have become if he'd embraced chaos instead of imposing order.

This dynamic makes the Joker more than just a villain. He's a philosophical challenge to everything Batman represents. Their conflict isn't just physical but ideological. The Joker wants to prove that anyone can be broken, that civilization is a joke, that the only honest response to existence is to laugh at the absurdity. Batman's refusal to kill the Joker, despite the countless deaths the Joker causes, becomes a statement about maintaining principles even when they seem futile.

The painted smile is central to all of this. The Joker grins while committing atrocities, finding genuine amusement in suffering and chaos. But the grin also suggests pain, the rictus of someone laughing because the alternative is screaming. Different interpretations emphasize different aspects of this duality, but all recognize that the smile is the character's most essential feature.

In broader culture, the Joker has become a symbol appropriated by various groups and movements. Anonymous and other hacktivist groups adopted Joker imagery to represent their opposition to established systems. Some incel and mass shooter manifestos referenced the character, seeing him as validation for their grievances and violence. Mental health advocates pointed to portrayals like Phoenix's as highlighting societal failures to support vulnerable people.

These appropriations demonstrate the danger of creating compelling villains. The Joker is designed to be charismatic, funny, and philosophically interesting. This makes him attractive as a symbol, but it also means he can be misinterpreted or deliberately misused. The character's rejection of social norms and embrace of violence can be read as liberating rather than horrifying if you're predisposed to see it that way.

The Joker endures because he represents something fundamental about the human condition that we recognize but usually suppress: the knowledge that meaning is fragile, that social order is constructed rather than natural, that chaos is always one breakdown away. The clown makeup makes this existential terror palatable, even entertaining. We can engage with these dark ideas because they're presented by a character in costume, performing for our amusement.

But the performance is the point. The Joker shows us that we're all performing, all wearing masks, all pretending that life makes sense when it fundamentally doesn't. The painted smile is the most honest expression possible: acknowledgment that the performance is absurd, that the mask is all there is, and that the only appropriate response is to laugh while everything burns.

The Joker is the ultimate killer clown because he understood something the others didn't: the horror isn't in the killing. The horror is in the smile.

Chapter Eight

Pennywise: The Shape-Shifting Terror

Pennywise the Dancing Clown is not human. This is the fundamental truth that separates Pennywise from other killer clowns. The Joker, Art the Clown, even John Wayne Gacy wearing his Pogo costume—these are humans who adopt clown personas. Pennywise is something ancient and alien that chooses to appear as a clown because that form is effective for hunting. The clown is not a disguise. It's bait.

Stephen King introduced Pennywise in his 1986 novel "It," and in doing so created perhaps the most influential killer clown in horror fiction. The novel tells the story of seven children in Derry, Maine, who encounter a supernatural entity that awakens every 27 years to feed on the town's children. The entity can assume any form, exploiting the fears of its victims. But its preferred form, the one it returns to most frequently, is Pennywise the Dancing Clown.

Why a clown? King understood that clowns occupy a unique psychological space. They're supposed to attract children, to be friendly and non-threatening. But they're also inherently unsettling, operating in that uncanny valley between human and not-quite-human. A predator disguised as a clown is perfectly camouflaged because clowns are already designed to lure children while triggering adult suspicion. The form is ideal for a creature that feeds on fear and flesh.

The novel's Pennywise is described in vivid, disturbing detail. The white face with the bright orange pompoms of hair. The baggy silk suit in orange and silver. The white gloves. The red smile stretched impossibly wide. The eyes that glow yellow when the creature's true nature surfaces. Every element of the description contributes to making Pennywise both recognizable as a clown and fundamentally wrong, a clown that doesn't obey the laws of physics or biology.

King's genius was in making Pennywise simultaneously playful and predatory. The creature greets children cheerfully, offers balloons, performs tricks. It speaks in the exaggerated, performative manner of children's entertainers. But underneath the performance is ancient malice, hunger, and something that delights in suffering for its own sake. Pennywise enjoys the hunt, the fear, the moment before the kill. The clown persona isn't just camouflage; it's how the creature experiences joy.

The novel explores how Pennywise operates through multiple encounters with different children. Each sees the clown differently based on their individual fears and psychology. For some, Pennywise is amusing until it suddenly isn't. For others, it's immediately terrifying. The entity adapts its performance to each victim, understanding instinctively how to manipulate and terrify. This adaptability makes it a perfect predator and a perfect metaphor for childhood trauma that takes whatever form will hurt most.

The creature's true form is revealed only glimpses—something spider-like, something with too many limbs, something that exists partially outside normal space and time. But significantly, even when the children confront it in its lair and force it to show its true nature, it keeps returning to the Pennywise form. The clown isn't just one shape among many. It's the entity's preferred self-presentation, the form it's most comfortable inhabiting.

This suggests something disturbing: Pennywise isn't merely using the clown as a tool. On some level, it is a clown, or has become one through centuries of using that form. The performance has consumed the performer, or perhaps there never was a distinction between them. The clown is the monster and the monster is the clown, inseparably fused.

The 1990 television miniseries brought Pennywise to millions of viewers through Tim Curry's iconic performance. Working within the constraints of early 1990s television special effects and content restrictions, Curry created a Pennywise that was charming and horrifying in equal measure. His Pennywise could shift from playful to menacing in seconds, his voice changing from friendly performer to demonic threat without the physical appearance changing at all.

Curry understood that the horror of Pennywise wasn't in the monster makeup or special effects. It was in the performance itself, in the way the clown's cheerfulness conceals and reveals malice simultaneously. His Pennywise smiles while threatening, jokes while hunting, maintains the performance even when dropping the pretense of friendliness. The clown persona is so deeply embedded that it doesn't disappear when the creature attacks. It warps, becoming a nightmarish inversion of what clowns are supposed to be.

The miniseries had significant limitations due to its medium and era. The special effects haven't aged well. The need to edit for television meant toning down the novel's more extreme horror. The ending, constrained by budget and the limitations of practical effects, failed to capture the cosmic terror of the book's climax. But Curry's performance transcended these limitations, creating an image of Pennywise that defined the character for a generation.

Curry's Pennywise became culturally iconic in ways that extended far beyond the miniseries itself. Images of him in the sewer drain, offering Georgie a balloon, became instantly recognizable symbols of killer clown horror. The voice, with its exaggerated friendliness masking obvious threat, was mimicked and parodied endlessly. An entire generation developed coulrophobia or had existing clown fears intensified by watching Curry's performance.

The famous line "We all float down here" became one of horror's most memorable catchphrases. The phrase works on multiple levels: literal (the entity makes its victims float), metaphorical (everyone eventually dies), and psychological (we all surrender to forces beyond our control). Delivered in Pennywise's performative voice, it becomes both invitation and threat, promise and warning.

The 2017 film adaptation took a radically different approach. Director Andy Muschietti and actor Bill Skarsgård created a Pennywise that was more overtly monstrous, less charming, and more clearly inhuman from the start. This version's face has slightly wrong proportions, with eyes that point in different directions and a mouth that opens too wide, revealing too many teeth. The performance is more alien, more insectoid, suggesting something that's imitating a clown rather than being one.

Skarsgård's Pennywise is deeply unsettling in different ways than Curry's. Where Curry emphasized the performance and the threat hidden behind friendliness, Skarsgård emphasizes wrongness. This Pennywise doesn't quite move like a human should. Its facial expressions are exaggerated beyond what human musculature can produce. Its voice has layers, harmonics that suggest multiple entities speaking simultaneously. Even when it's trying to be appealing, it's clearly wrong.

The film's depiction of Pennywise's shapeshifting is more explicit and disturbing than the miniseries could achieve. The creature transforms fluidly, grotesquely, its body contorting in ways that violate physics and biology. But significantly, it always returns to the Pennywise form. Even when appearing as a leper, a painting come to life, or a giant creature from a child's nightmares, elements of the clown persist. The red nose appears on the leper. The clown makeup bleeds through other forms. Pennywise is the default, the base state.

This visual persistence reinforces the idea that Pennywise isn't disguising itself as a clown. The clown is what it is. The other forms are variations, but the clown is fundamental to the entity's identity. This makes it more disturbing than a simple shapeshifter. This is a creature that has chosen to be a clown, that prefers to be a clown, that returns to being a clown whenever possible.

The 2017 film and its 2019 sequel "It Chapter Two" explored aspects of Pennywise's nature and history that the miniseries couldn't address. The entity is revealed to be ancient, predating human civilization, arriving on Earth millions of years ago. It has fed on humans throughout history, adapting its form to whatever would be most effective in each era. But in modern Derry, it has settled on Pennywise as its primary manifestation.

This choice is significant. With all of human history and culture to draw from, with infinite possible forms, the entity chooses a clown. This suggests that clowns are universally effective as lures and sources of fear. Children are attracted to them. Adults are unsettled by them. The form bridges the gap between generations, working on both the young victims and the adult survivors who return to face their childhood terror.

The Pennywise form also allows the entity to operate openly. A clown walking through town, standing near a storm drain, appearing at a carnival or festival—none of this seems out of place. The disguise isn't that Pennywise looks harmless. It's that Pennywise looks like it belongs, like it's supposed to be there. The clown costume provides cover to operate in public spaces without triggering immediate alarm.

Pennywise's relationship with fear is central to understanding the character. The entity doesn't just kill; it feeds on fear first, salting the meat as King describes it. The elaborate performances, the psychological torture, the extended stalking—all of this serves to maximize terror before the kill. Pennywise needs its victims to be afraid, and the clown form is perfectly designed to generate that fear.

This is where the character becomes metatextual. Pennywise is a creature that feeds on fear, appearing in a form designed to frighten, in a horror novel designed to frighten readers. The character breaks the fourth wall in subtle ways, acknowledging that it exists to scare, that this is its purpose and joy. When Pennywise performs for its victims, it's also performing for us, the readers and viewers, aware that we're watching and meant to be disturbed.

The balloon is Pennywise's signature prop, appearing in nearly every encounter with the entity. Red balloons float where they shouldn't, appear in impossible places, multiply impossibly. They're innocent objects transformed into harbingers of doom. The balloon becomes a calling card, a warning, a promise. Its presence means Pennywise is near, that the performance is about to begin, that someone is about to die.

King's novel and its adaptations explore the idea that Pennywise can be defeated only by children, or by adults who can reconnect with their childhood selves. The entity is vulnerable to imagination, to belief, to the conviction that it can be harmed. This suggests that Pennywise exists partially in the realm of the imaginary, that it's as much psychological as physical. The clown form reflects this liminal status—real enough to kill but also performative, theatrical, existing on the boundary between reality and nightmare.

The creature's 27-year cycle creates an interesting pattern. Pennywise awakens, feeds, then sleeps, then returns. This rhythm suggests something almost seasonal, natural, despite the entity's alien nature. The cycle allows King to explore how trauma echoes across time, how childhood fears persist into adulthood, how some horrors don't stay buried.

Pennywise has influenced countless subsequent killer clowns in fiction and media. The specific image of a clown in a sewer drain, offering something to a child, has been referenced, parodied, and copied endlessly. The character established templates for how killer clowns should look, sound, and behave that continue to influence horror creators decades later.

But Pennywise's ultimate legacy is making explicit what was always implicit about clowns: they're predators wearing the costume of entertainers, hunters using fun as camouflage, ancient terrors dressed in silly suits. The painted smile hides rows of teeth. The friendly performance masks malevolent intent. The balloon is a lure. And we all float down here eventually, caught by the creature that learned long ago that the best disguise is the one that's already unsettling, already wrong, already halfway to nightmare.

The clown doesn't need to hide what it is. It just needs to smile.

Chapter Nine

Art the Clown: The Silent Sadist

Art the Clown is different. Where the Joker philosophizes and Pennywise feeds on cosmic terror, Art simply kills. Brutally, creatively, relentlessly. He doesn't speak, doesn't explain, doesn't monologue about his motivations. He just appears, smiles that horrible black-and-white smile, and begins inflicting suffering that goes far beyond what's necessary to kill. Art the Clown is pure sadism in clown form, and that purity makes him uniquely terrifying.

Created by filmmaker Damien Leone, Art first appeared in the short film "The 9th Circle" (2008) before becoming the central antagonist in "All Hallows' Eve" (2013) and the "Terrifier" films (2016, 2022). Unlike the Joker or Pennywise, Art has no origin story, no explanation, no context. He exists. He kills. That's all we know and possibly all there is to know.

The character's design is deliberately unsettling. Art wears a black and white clown costume that's both stark and filthy, suggesting a performer who's been working too long without cleaning up. His face paint is similarly monochromatic, creating a mime-like appearance that's less colorful than traditional clowns but somehow more disturbing. The black lipstick drawn over his mouth creates an exaggerated smile that doesn't match his actual expression, making his face unreadable in a way that even other clown characters aren't.

His eyes are perhaps his most disturbing feature. They're expressive and intelligent, communicating clearly despite his complete silence. Art's eyes show amusement, curiosity, mock sadness, exaggerated surprise—a full range of emotions, but all in service of his sadistic games. He watches his victims with the attention of someone truly interested in their suffering, studying their fear like a connoisseur evaluating fine wine.

The silence is crucial to Art's effectiveness. Most horror villains speak, revealing their personalities, motivations, and weaknesses through dialogue. Art's complete muteness makes him unknowable. We cannot gauge his intelligence or mental state through speech. We cannot predict what he'll do next based on what he says. The silence creates a void that our imaginations fill with worst-case scenarios, and Art consistently proves our imaginations were too optimistic.

But Art isn't silent in the way Michael Myers is silent. Myers is blank, emotionless, mechanical. Art is highly expressive, communicating through exaggerated mime gestures, theatrical movements, and facial expressions that his makeup partially obscures. He performs silently, treating murder as slapstick comedy where only he understands the joke. This performance makes him more disturbing than a blank killer would be because it suggests consciousness, choice, delight.

Art takes visible pleasure in his work. He smiles genuinely while killing, not with the forced painted smile but with evident enjoyment in his eyes and body language. He's having fun. The torture and murder aren't means to an end; they are the end. He kills because he enjoys killing, and he clearly wants his victims to know this before they die.

The character's violence is extreme even by horror film standards. The "Terrifier" films feature kills that are prolonged, detailed, and genuinely difficult to watch. Art doesn't simply murder; he tortures, mutilates, and desecrates. He uses whatever tools are available, improvising elaborate deaths with whatever he finds. A hacksaw, a scalpel, chemicals, blunt objects—everything becomes a murder weapon in Art's hands.

One particularly infamous scene involves Art sawing a woman in half vertically, starting from between her legs. The scene is shot unflinchingly, showing the process in graphic detail, making the audience endure the victim's suffering alongside her. It's not violence for shock value; it's violence as Art's expression of who he is. This is what he does. This is what he enjoys. And the film forces us to witness it.

This extremity has made Art the Clown controversial. Critics argue that the violence is gratuitous, that it crosses lines that even horror should respect, that it celebrates sadism rather than critiquing it. Fans counter that Art represents horror stripped to its essential elements: fear, pain, death, delivered without pretense or justification. The character doesn't ask for sympathy or understanding. He exists as pure antagonist, pure threat.

Art's relationship with his victims is distinctive. He often toys with them before killing, playing cruel games, offering false hope, mimicking their terror with exaggerated expressions of fear. He'll pretend to be scared himself, cowering and trembling in mockery of his victim's genuine terror. Then he'll drop the act and attack. The psychological torture compounds the physical, making the experience worse than simple murder would be.

The character's physicality is remarkable. Actor David Howard Thornton brings a background in mime and physical theater to the role, giving Art a distinctive movement style that's simultaneously graceful and grotesque. Art moves with exaggerated precision, every gesture deliberate and theatrical. He skips, dances, performs elaborate pantomimes. This balletic quality makes his violence more disturbing because it shows control, intention, artistry in the worst possible sense.

Art's facial expressions do most of his communication. Thornton's performance involves constant, exaggerated reactions to everything happening around him. Art's face shows delight at finding new victims, mock concern when they cry, exaggerated surprise when they fight back, childlike joy when he finds new tools to use. These expressions would be comical in other contexts, but here they create a disconnect between the emotional display and the horrific actions, amplifying the disturbing effect.

The character's apparent indestructibility adds another layer of horror. Art sustains injuries that should kill him but keeps functioning. He's shot, beaten, burned, and seemingly killed multiple times, only to reappear later unharmed or rapidly healing. The films offer no explanation for this. He's not explicitly supernatural like Pennywise, but he's clearly not human either. He exists in an ambiguous space where the normal rules don't apply.

This invulnerability makes Art an unstoppable force in ways that even supernatural killers often aren't. You cannot reason with him because he doesn't speak. You cannot kill him because he doesn't stay dead. You cannot predict his actions because he operates from motivations that aren't explained or possibly don't exist. The only option is to run, and running rarely works.

Art's use of props and costumes adds to his theatrical presentation. He's often seen carrying a black garbage bag containing his tools and weapons. He changes costumes occasionally, appearing in different outfits while maintaining his core clown aesthetic. In "Terrifier 2," he wears a Santa suit for a sequence, merging another childhood symbol with his sadistic nature. The costume changes suggest awareness of his own presentation, an understanding that the performance matters.

The films depict Art operating primarily on Halloween, using the holiday as cover. A clown walking the streets on Halloween night attracts no attention. He blends perfectly into the environment, just another person in costume. This allows him to hunt openly, approaching victims without raising alarm until it's too late. The holiday setting also adds thematic weight: Halloween is when we play with fear, when we dress as monsters and pretend. Art makes the pretense real.

Art's relationship with his victims varies. Some he kills quickly, almost as afterthoughts. Others he focuses on, clearly selecting them for extended attention. The criteria for this selection aren't clear. Sometimes it seems based on opportunity, sometimes on the victim's reactions to him, sometimes on factors only Art understands. This unpredictability means no one is safe, but also no one knows if they're a primary target until Art decides.

The character's popularity has grown significantly, particularly after "Terrifier 2" became a surprise hit in 2022. The film, made on a relatively small budget, achieved significant box office success and cultural penetration. Reports of audience members fainting or vomiting during screenings generated publicity and curiosity. Art the Clown became a phenomenon, with Halloween costumes, fan art, and extensive online discussion.

This popularity is interesting given the character's complete lack of sympathetic qualities. Art has no tragic backstory, no redeeming features, no complexity beyond his sadism. He exists purely to cause suffering. Yet audiences respond to him, finding something compelling in his pure villainy. Perhaps it's the honesty of it—Art doesn't pretend to be anything other than what he is. He's evil without justification, and there's something almost refreshing about a villain who doesn't ask for understanding.

The silence remains his most defining feature. In a media landscape filled with chatty villains who explain their plans and motivations, Art's muteness makes him an outlier. We get no monologues about society or chaos or revenge. We get only actions, and those actions speak clearly enough. Art kills because he wants to, because he can, because he enjoys it. No further explanation is necessary or forthcoming.

This lack of motivation actually makes Art more frightening for many viewers. Villains with understandable motivations can be reasoned with, predicted, potentially stopped by addressing their goals. Art has no goals beyond the immediate act of killing. He's not trying to prove a point or achieve an objective. He's simply being what he is, and what he is doesn't need justification.

The character represents a specific type of killer clown: the one who uses the costume purely as camouflage and aesthetic choice rather than as expression of deeper themes. Art doesn't philosophize about chaos like the Joker. He doesn't feed on fear like Pennywise. He's a sadistic killer who happens to dress as a clown because it's effective and because, perhaps, it amuses him to corrupt symbols of childhood joy.

Art the Clown has influenced the broader killer clown genre by demonstrating that less can be more. No supernatural powers are necessary (though Art's durability suggests something inhuman). No complex origin story is required. No dialogue or explanation needed. Just a clown, some weapons, and the willingness to depict extreme violence unflinchingly. This stripped-down approach has spawned imitators and influenced how other horror creators approach clown characters.

The character also represents how far clown horror has come from its earlier incarnations. Art couldn't have existed in the 1980s or even the 1990s. The cultural acceptance of extreme violence in horror films, the platforms allowing independent horror to find audiences, the established association between clowns and terror—all of these had to be in place for Art to work.

Art the Clown is what you get when you remove everything from the killer clown except the killing. No philosophy, no cosmic horror, no psychological complexity. Just a silent figure in black and white makeup who smiles while inflicting unimaginable suffering. The painted grin isn't hiding anything deeper. The smile is the message. Art is having fun, and your terror is the entertainment.

In his silence, Art speaks volumes about what clowns have become in our cultural imagination. They're no longer figures of joy or even figures with comprehensible motivations. They're simply threats, predators wearing costumes that used to mean something innocent but now only signal danger. The transformation is complete, and Art the Clown is its purest expression.

He doesn't need to explain himself. The smile says everything.

Chapter Ten

John Wayne Gacy: The Real-Life Killer Clown

John Wayne Gacy was not a fictional monster. He was a real man who raped and murdered at least 33 young men and boys between 1972 and 1978. He buried most of them in the crawl space beneath his house in suburban Chicago. And he was known in his community as Pogo the Clown, a beloved children's entertainer who performed at parties, parades, and charity events. This juxtaposition between public persona and private horror makes Gacy perhaps the most terrifying killer clown of all, because he actually existed.

Gacy's story is crucial to understanding how clowns became associated with horror in popular culture. Before Gacy's arrest in 1978, clowns were still primarily seen as harmless entertainers. After Gacy, that perception became impossible to maintain. Here was proof that the painted smile could hide a monster, that the costume designed to delight children could be worn by someone who preyed on them. Gacy didn't just kill people while happening to dress as a clown occasionally. The clown persona was integral to who he was and how he operated.

Born in 1942 in Chicago, Gacy had a troubled childhood marked by physical abuse from his father and confusion about his sexuality in an era when being gay was stigmatized and criminalized. As an adult, he presented himself as a pillar of the community: a successful businessman, active in local Democratic Party politics, a married father who hosted elaborate neighborhood parties and barbecues. He was well-liked, respected, someone people trusted.

The clown persona emerged as part of this public image. Gacy created the character of Pogo the Clown and later added a second character, Patches. He designed his own costumes and makeup, joining a local clown club and performing at children's hospitals, charity events, and neighborhood gatherings. Photographs from this period show Gacy in full clown makeup and costume, surrounded by smiling children, looking every bit the wholesome entertainer.

But the makeup Gacy designed was subtly wrong. Where most clowns used rounded, soft shapes in their face paint, Gacy's design featured sharp angles. His painted mouth had pointed corners that extended past where a natural smile would end. The eyebrows were severely arched. The overall effect was less friendly than traditional clown makeup, though apparently not enough to alarm the parents who hired him or the children he entertained.

Gacy's murders followed a pattern. He would lure young men and teenage boys to his house with offers of construction work (he owned a contracting business), alcohol, or simply friendly conversation. Once inside, he would overpower them, often using what he called his "handcuff trick" to restrain them under the guise of demonstrating a magic illusion. Then he would rape, torture, and eventually strangle them. He buried most bodies in the crawl space beneath his house. When that space ran out, he disposed of bodies in a nearby river.

The victims were often runaways, young gay men, or others on society's margins—people whose disappearances might not be immediately noticed or vigorously investigated. Gacy exploited this invisibility, continuing to kill for years while maintaining his public image as a community leader and entertainer. He threw parties where guests ate and drank mere feet above the decomposing bodies buried beneath the house.

The duality of Gacy's life was extreme but not unprecedented. Serial killers often maintain outward normalcy while committing atrocities in private. What made Gacy unique was the clown persona, which added another layer of deception and made his crimes feel particularly perverse. The costume designed to make children feel safe was worn by someone who represented their worst nightmare.

Gacy was arrested in December 1978 after police investigating the disappearance of 15-year-old Robert Piest obtained a search warrant for his house. The search revealed evidence of murders, and eventually Gacy confessed, directing police to the bodies buried beneath his house and providing information about those disposed of elsewhere. The excavation of the crawl space became a media sensation, with news coverage showing workers removing body after body from beneath the suburban home.

The clown connection was irresistible to media coverage. Headlines screamed about the "Killer Clown" even though Gacy had committed his murders as himself, not while in costume. But the juxtaposition was too powerful to ignore: respected community member by day, children's entertainer on weekends, serial killer in private. The images of Gacy in his Pogo costume were shown alongside mugshots and crime scene photos, forever linking the cheerful clown appearance with the brutal reality of his crimes.

The trial of John Wayne Gacy was a media spectacle. Prosecutors detailed the horrific nature of his crimes, the torture he inflicted, the lives he destroyed. Gacy's defense attempted to argue insanity, claiming that only a madman could commit such acts. But the prosecution successfully portrayed Gacy as calculating and aware of his actions, someone who carefully planned his crimes and worked to avoid detection. The jury agreed, convicting him of 33 murders and sentencing him to death.

During his 14 years on death row, Gacy maintained his innocence despite his earlier confessions. He gave interviews, painted numerous artworks (many featuring clowns), and continued to attract attention. His paintings became controversial collectibles, with some people buying them as macabre artifacts while others found the very existence of such a market disturbing. The clown paintings were particularly sought after, images of Pogo and other clown characters rendered by the hands that had strangled 33 people.

These paintings are unsettling not because of anything overtly horrific in their content but because of who created them. They're often technically competent, colorful, even cheerful in appearance. But knowing they were painted by a serial killer transforms them into something sinister. The painted smile on the canvas becomes a reminder of the painted smile Gacy wore while being photographed with children, while maintaining his public persona, while his victims decomposed beneath his house.

Gacy was executed by lethal injection in 1994. His final words were reportedly "Kiss my ass," defiant to the end. His death did not end his cultural impact. If anything, it cemented his place in American cultural consciousness as the definitive real-life killer clown, the proof that our fears about clowns had basis in reality.

The psychological profile that emerged of Gacy showed a man with narcissistic traits, a need for control and domination, and complete lack of empathy for his victims. He was intelligent enough to maintain his double life for years, manipulating those around him into seeing only what he wanted them to see. The clown persona was part of this manipulation, a way of appearing harmless and community-oriented while being anything but.

Some psychologists have noted that Gacy's clown performances may have served multiple purposes beyond simple camouflage. The act of entertaining children while harboring such dark desires may have been psychologically gratifying in itself, a form of control or dominance. Alternatively, the performance might have been an attempt to convince himself of his own normalcy, to prove that he could be the person he presented himself as being.

The impact of Gacy on cultural perceptions of clowns cannot be overstated. Before his arrest, coulrophobia existed but was relatively uncommon and not culturally validated. After Gacy, fear of clowns became understandable, even expected. Parents became more cautious about clown entertainers. Background checks became standard for those working with children. The automatic trust that might once have been extended to someone in a clown costume evaporated.

Stephen King was writing "It" during the period of Gacy's trial and execution. While King has stated that his fear of clowns predated Gacy, the timing is significant. Pennywise appeared in cultural consciousness when the real-life killer clown was daily news. The fictional and real monsters reinforced each other, creating a perfect storm that transformed clowns from entertainers to figures of terror.

Gacy's case also influenced how serial killers are understood and portrayed in popular culture. He demonstrated that monsters don't look like monsters. They look like your neighbor, your coworker, the guy who volunteers at community events. They smile in photographs. They maintain relationships. They function in society while committing atrocities. The clown costume became a symbol of this deception, the ultimate mask hiding the ultimate predator.

True crime media has extensively covered Gacy, producing documentaries, books, podcasts, and dramatizations. Each retelling emphasizes the clown connection, often using images of Gacy in costume even when discussing aspects of his crimes that had nothing to do with his performances. The clown has become inseparable from the killer, defining how he's remembered and discussed.

Gacy's house was demolished after the bodies were removed. The property was sold and a new house built on the site. But the address is known, and the location remains a dark landmark in Chicago's history. Similarly, the crawl space where the bodies were found has become a symbol in discussions of evil, of how horror can exist beneath ordinary suburban normalcy, literally underfoot while life continues above.

The victims of John Wayne Gacy deserve remembrance beyond their association with their killer. They were young men with lives, families, futures that were stolen from them. Their names: Timothy McCoy, John Butkovitch, Darrell Samson, Randall Reffett, Samuel Stapleton, Michael Bonnin, William Carroll, James Haakenson, Rick Johnston, Kenneth Parker, Michael Marino, William Bundy, Francis Wayne Alexander, Gregory Godzik, John Szyc, Jon Prestidge, Matthew Bowman, Robert Gilroy, John Mowery, Russell Nelson, Robert Winch, Tommy Boling, David Talsma, William Kindred, Timothy O'Rourke, Frank Landingin, James Mazzara, Robert Piest, and five who remain unidentified. Each was a person, not just a statistic in the crimes of John Wayne Gacy.

But the cultural legacy is undeniable. Gacy proved that the killer clown was not just fiction, not just exaggeration, not just coulrophobic paranoia. He was real. He smiled for photographs. He entertained children. He wore the costume and the makeup and used the trust that costume generated to conceal unspeakable evil.

Every killer clown that came after—in fiction, in film, in Halloween costumes, in the 2016 sightings—exists in the shadow of John Wayne Gacy. He made the archetype real, validating every instinct that said the painted smile might be hiding something monstrous. Pogo the Clown became the nightmare that proved our fears were not irrational.

The real monster wore makeup. The painted smile hid a predator. And the clown was never innocent again.

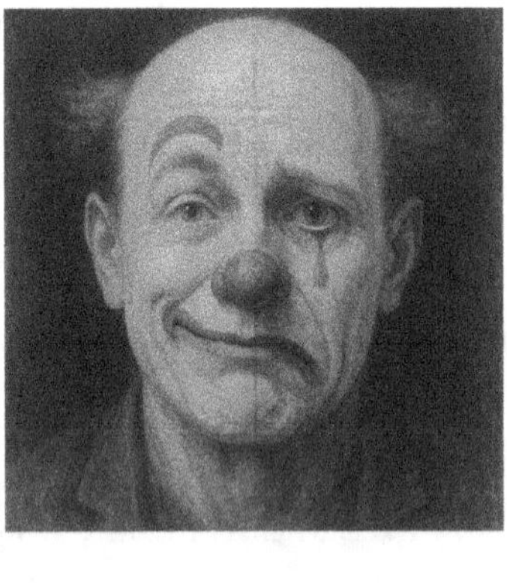

Chapter Eleven

Twisty the Clown: Tragedy and Terror

Twisty the Clown appeared in season four of "American Horror Story: Freak Show" (2014) and became one of the series' most memorable and disturbing characters despite appearing in only a handful of episodes. Portrayed by John Carroll Lynch, Twisty represented a different approach to the killer clown archetype: a monster created by cruelty rather than born evil, a tragic figure whose appearance matched the horror of what had been done to him.

Twisty's visual design is immediately striking and deeply unsettling. He wears a filthy, tattered clown costume that suggests decades of wear without cleaning. His face paint is smeared and faded, applied over what appears to be a grotesque prosthetic mask covering the lower half of his face. The mask itself is crude, clearly handmade, with a painted-on smile that doesn't move. When the mask is eventually removed, the horror beneath is revealed: Twisty's jaw is missing, destroyed by a self-inflicted shotgun blast that failed to kill him.

The character's backstory, revealed midway through the season, recontextualizes everything we've seen. Twisty was a gentle, simple-minded man who worked as a clown for a traveling circus in the 1940s. He genuinely loved entertaining children and was good at his job. But other performers, jealous of his popularity, spread rumors that he was a child molester. The accusations destroyed him. He was fired, shunned, unable to work. Unable to cope with the injustice and having lost everything that gave his life meaning, Twisty attempted suicide by shooting himself in the mouth.

The suicide attempt failed catastrophically, destroying his lower jaw but leaving him alive. Unable to speak, horribly disfigured, rejected by society, Twisty's mind broke completely. He created the crude mask to hide his destroyed face and began kidnapping children, holding them prisoner in an old bus. In his fractured mind, he was still a performer, still entertaining children, still serving his purpose. The children he kidnapped were terrified, but Twisty couldn't understand why. He was just trying to make them happy.

This backstory creates uncomfortable sympathy for a character who does monstrous things. Twisty is a killer and a kidnapper, genuinely dangerous and frightening. But he's also a victim, someone destroyed by cruelty who literally cannot comprehend what he's become. The tragedy doesn't excuse the horror, but it complicates it in ways that most killer clown characters don't.

The character's inability to speak (due to his missing jaw) creates parallels with Art the Clown's deliberate silence, but the effect is completely different. Art's silence is predatory, enhancing his menace. Twisty's silence is pathetic, a physical manifestation of how society silenced him, how he cannot explain or defend himself, how he's trapped in his own damaged mind without the ability to communicate.

Twisty's performance of being a clown is heartbreaking in its earnestness. He still does tricks, still tries to make people laugh, still believes he's entertaining even as his captives scream and try to escape. The disconnect between his perception and reality is total. In his mind, he's Twisty the Clown, beloved performer. In reality, he's a nightmare, a monster wearing the ruins of who he used to be.

The show uses Twisty to explore how society creates monsters. The false accusations that destroyed his life, the complete lack of support or help after his suicide attempt, the rejection that left him with nowhere to go and no way to function—all of these are indictments of how we treat the vulnerable and different. Twisty became a killer not because he was evil but because he was broken by a system that had no place for him.

This social commentary distinguishes Twisty from other killer clowns. The Joker embraces chaos philosophically. Pennywise is an alien monster. Art is pure sadism. But Twisty is a critique, a demonstration of how cruelty and injustice create violence, how destroying someone's identity and purpose can shatter them into something dangerous.

The character's appearance became iconic despite his limited screen time. The crude mask with its fixed grin, the filthy costume, the wild hair, the imposing physical presence—all of it created an image that haunted viewers. The reveal of what lay beneath the mask became one of the series' most disturbing moments, not because of gore (though the destroyed jaw is graphic) but because of what it represented.

The mask itself is symbolically important. It's literally a false face, a crude attempt to reconstruct what was destroyed. But it can't truly hide the damage. The smile painted on the mask is garish and wrong, a mockery of what a smile should be. When Twisty wears it, he's attempting to restore his identity as a clown, to rebuild what was taken from him. But the reconstruction is imperfect, damaged, more disturbing than honest disfigurement would be.

Twisty's murders are brutal but not sadistic. He kills to protect his captive "audience" or to eliminate threats, not because he enjoys suffering. This distinguishes him from Art or even the Joker. He's dangerous and violent, but there's no pleasure in it. He's simply doing what his broken mind tells him is necessary. This makes him perhaps more tragic than terrifying, though he achieves both.

The character's fate reinforces the tragedy. He's eventually killed by another character, Edward Mordrake, a ghost with a demonic face on the back of his head who collects tortured souls. Mordrake hears Twisty's story and, in a moment of mercy, kills him and takes him into his ghostly carnival. Twisty's final expression, visible even through the mask, is relief. Death is release from the nightmare his life became.

After death, Twisty appears in later seasons of "American Horror Story" as a ghost or spirit, still performing, still clowning, but now freed from the pain and confusion that defined his life. In these appearances, he seems almost peaceful, or at least no longer tortured. The afterlife has given him what life couldn't: purpose and identity without suffering.

"American Horror Story" used Twisty to explore themes of disability, social cruelty, and how society treats those who don't fit conventional norms. His intellectual disability, his poverty, his unconventional career choice as a clown—all of these made him vulnerable to the malicious rumors that destroyed him. The show suggests that monsters are often made, not born, created by systems and people who reject and harm those they consider other.

The character also examines the clown as an identity rather than just a costume. For Twisty, being a clown wasn't what he did; it was who he was. When that identity was stripped away by false accusations, he ceased to exist as himself. The suicide attempt was an attempt to end the unbearable existence of being Twisty without being a clown. When it failed, he reconstructed himself as best he could, creating a damaged version of the identity he'd lost.

This raises questions about how we construct identity and what happens when external forces destroy it. Twisty literally rebuilt his face (with the crude mask) and his identity (as a performer) after both were destroyed. But the reconstruction was imperfect, wrong, monstrous. The show asks whether this is Twisty's failure or society's—whether the monster is the man who couldn't properly rebuild himself or the system that destroyed him in the first place.

Twisty's relationship with children is particularly complex and disturbing. He genuinely believes he's entertaining them, making them happy, giving them the performances he used to give. He cannot process their terror as terror. In his damaged mind, screams might be laughter, fear might be excitement, captivity might be audience participation. This delusional state makes him both more pathetic and more dangerous.

The character influenced how subsequent horror creators approached killer clowns. Twisty demonstrated that the archetype could carry emotional and thematic weight beyond simple scares. A killer clown could be a tragedy, a social commentary, a meditation on identity and cruelty, while still functioning as an effective horror antagonist. The two modes—tragic victim and terrifying monster—could coexist in the same character.

John Carroll Lynch's performance was crucial to achieving this balance. He brought genuine pathos to Twisty, making the character's confusion and pain palpable even through the mask and makeup. The physicality was imposing and frightening, but the emotional core was heartbreaking. Lynch showed that even without dialogue, a performer could convey complex emotional states and create a character that transcended the limitations of the grotesque costume.

The public response to Twisty was mixed and revealing. Some viewers found the character too disturbing, particularly the reveal of his destroyed face. Others connected with the tragedy, seeing Twisty as a victim rather than a villain. This division reflected broader questions about sympathy, responsibility, and whether understanding what created a monster means excusing what the monster does.

Twisty's legacy in killer clown lore is secure. He proved that the archetype could be more than just scary, that it could provoke thought and feeling beyond simple fear. The character demonstrated that clowns could be symbols not just of chaos or evil but of how cruelty creates violence, how society's rejection transforms people into the monsters it then fears.

The crude mask has become an iconic image in horror culture, frequently referenced, parodied, and copied. It represents the idea of damaged identity, of attempts to reconstruct what's been destroyed, of the false face that can't quite hide the trauma beneath. The fixed smile painted on the mask is a lie, but it's a lie Twisty desperately needs to believe.

In the end, Twisty is perhaps the saddest of the major killer clowns. The Joker chose chaos. Pennywise is evil by nature. Art enjoys suffering. But Twisty just wanted to make children laugh, to have purpose, to be who he was before cruelty destroyed him. The tragedy is that he achieved none of it, that his attempt to reclaim his identity only created a monster, that the smile he wore was painted over ruin.

The character asks us to consider where our monsters come from, whether they're born or made, and what responsibility we bear for creating them. Twisty didn't choose to become a killer. He was pushed into it by false accusations, social rejection, and a failed suicide that left him shattered in every way. The horror isn't just what he became. It's that he became it because of what was done to him.

The painted smile on the crude mask hides a destroyed face. But it also hides a destroyed life, a destroyed identity, a destroyed soul. Twisty the Clown is a reminder that sometimes the scariest monsters are the ones we create through our own cruelty, rejection, and failure to help those who need it most.

The tragedy wears a mask. And beneath it, there's nothing but pain.

Chapter Twelve

Why Clowns Persist

The simplest answer to why clowns still exist is economic: they're cheap. A clown requires minimal equipment, no specialized venue, no expensive props beyond makeup and a costume that can be assembled for under a hundred dollars. For cash-strapped circuses, struggling children's hospitals, or budget birthday parties, clowns represent entertainment at minimal cost.

This economic reality explains why clowns survive in settings where they're clearly unwanted. Hospitals continue clown programs not because they're effective (many children are now terrified rather than comforted) but because the programs are already established, funded by donations earmarked specifically for that purpose, and eliminating them would require admitting failure. It's easier to keep sending clowns to pediatric wards than to return donor money and explain that clowns now traumatize more children than they help.

The regulatory vacuum surrounding clowning also ensures persistence. You don't need a license to be a clown. You don't need training, certification, background checks, or any credential whatsoever. You need face paint and a willingness to perform. This means clowns cannot be regulated out of existence the way other professions can be controlled or eliminated. Anyone can become a clown tomorrow simply by deciding to do so.

This lack of barrier to entry attracts precisely the wrong people. Legitimate performers with actual skills can find better opportunities in theater, stand-up comedy, or other entertainment fields that offer better pay and respect. Who chooses clowning in 2024? People with limited options, people attracted to the transgressive nature of a feared profession, people who enjoy making others uncomfortable, or people with concerning motivations who recognize that the clown costume provides access to children and public spaces while obscuring identity.

Professional clown organizations acknowledge this problem privately while defending their profession publicly. They know that the absence of gatekeeping means anyone can claim to be a clown, including people who damage the profession's already devastated reputation. But they cannot implement meaningful standards because clowning isn't a licensed profession. They can expel members from their organizations, but they cannot stop those people from continuing to perform as clowns.

The few remaining professional clowns fall into distinct categories. First are the legacy performers, people from circus families or who trained decades ago when clowning was still respected. They continue partly from stubbornness, partly because they've invested their entire lives in skills that aren't transferable, partly because they genuinely don't know what else to do. These performers are aging out, retiring or dying, not being replaced.

Second are the idealists who believe they can rehabilitate the clown's image through quality performance. They attend the remaining clown schools, study the history and techniques, approach it as serious art. These performers are naive but sincere. They believe that by being excellent clowns, by bringing genuine joy and skill to their performances, they can overcome decades of cultural conditioning. They're wrong, but their conviction is real.

Third are those who embrace the darkness. These performers recognize that clowns are now associated with horror and lean into it. They work Halloween events, horror conventions, haunted attractions. They've accepted that clowning as wholesome entertainment is dead and adapted to the new reality where clowns exist primarily to frighten. This is the growth sector of professional clowning, the only area where demand actually exists.

Fourth and most concerning are those attracted to clowning specifically because it's transgressive and provides cover for boundary violation. The clown costume has always permitted behavior that would be unacceptable otherwise. Invading personal space, touching without consent, ignoring when people say no, behaving unpredictably: all of this is supposedly acceptable because "that's what clowns do." People who want to engage in these behaviors while maintaining deniability are drawn to clowning.

This fourth category is why clowns cannot be rehabilitated. Even if ninety-nine clowns are well-intentioned performers, the hundredth uses the costume and cultural expectations to engage in predatory behavior. Parents cannot distinguish between them until it's too late. The costume itself has become a red flag, a warning sign, regardless of who wears it.

Circuses persist with clowns for structural reasons that have nothing to do with audience desire. The traditional circus format requires clowns to fill time during set changes, to provide comic relief between dangerous acts, to interact with audiences in ways that aerialists and acrobats cannot. Eliminating clowns would require restructuring the entire performance format, investing in new acts and transitions, fundamentally reimagining what a circus is.

Most circuses cannot afford this restructuring. They're already struggling financially, operating on thin margins, unable to invest in wholesale reinvention. So they keep the clowns despite knowing that significant portions of their audience find them unsettling rather than entertaining. It's cheaper to keep doing what they've always done than to change.

The few thriving circuses have indeed eliminated traditional clowns. Cirque du Soleil, the most commercially successful circus organization in the world, features no clowns in the traditional sense. Their shows include physical comedians and character performers, but these artists avoid clown makeup, clown costumes, and clown behavior patterns. They've proven that circus can exist and even thrive without clowns. But most circuses lack the resources to follow this model.

Regional and traveling circuses, the small operations that still tour rural areas and small towns, cling to clowns because they're cheap and traditional. These circuses serve older audiences who remember when clowns were acceptable, communities where cultural changes penetrate slowly, areas where people might not have seen the horror films and news coverage that transformed urban perceptions of clowns. In these markets, clowns still sometimes work as intended.

But even in these contexts, the effectiveness is declining. Children in rural areas have internet access. They've seen Pennywise. They know about killer clowns. The cultural shift has penetrated even the most isolated communities. Within another generation, even these last holdouts will likely abandon clowns simply because the audiences will no longer tolerate them.

Birthday party clowns represent a dying industry desperately trying to survive through rebranding. Many performers who once advertised as clowns now market themselves as "children's entertainers" or "party characters," avoiding the word entirely while still essentially performing clown functions. They've reduced the makeup, changed costumes to be less traditional, modified their acts to be less physical and invasive. They're trying to be clowns without being identifiable as clowns.

This rarely succeeds. Parents who are wary of clowns are also wary of anything that resembles a clown. The association is too strong. A performer in any kind of costume makeup doing physical comedy will trigger the same responses as a traditional clown would. The rebranding fools no one.

The internet has become the primary space where clown culture persists, but in forms the traditional clowning community barely recognizes. Online, clowning has split into incompatible factions. Traditional performers trying to preserve their art exist alongside horror enthusiasts, creepypasta creators, people making deliberately unsettling content, and those fascinated by clown aesthetics for reasons that have nothing to do with entertainment.

These groups share spaces but speak different languages. A professional clown posting about preserving traditional performance techniques receives responses from people whose profile pictures are horror clowns and whose interest is purely in the fear factor. The conversations are mutually incomprehensible. They're using the same word to mean completely different things.

Some performers have attempted to create "safe" clowning by eliminating all the elements that make clowns unsettling. No white face paint, no exaggerated features, no boundary violations, no unpredictability. What remains is essentially just a comedian in a colorful outfit. This might be effective entertainment, but it's not clowning in any meaningful sense. You cannot remove everything that makes a clown a clown and still claim to be preserving the tradition.

The academic study of clowning persists in theater programs, but increasingly as historical subject rather than living practice. Students learn about commedia dell'arte, study the great clowns of the past, analyze the techniques and traditions. But fewer are actually performing as clowns. The knowledge is being preserved the way we preserve information about obsolete technologies: interesting historically, not practically applicable.

Why doesn't society actively eliminate clowns? Several reasons. First, there's no mechanism to do so. You cannot ban people from wearing costumes and makeup. Any law attempting to prohibit clowning would face immediate First Amendment challenges and would likely be struck down. The government cannot eliminate a form of expression simply because people find it unsettling.

Second, there's no consensus that clowns should be eliminated. While many people fear or dislike clowns, others defend them, feel nostalgic about them, or believe they serve valuable functions. Any serious attempt to ban or eliminate clowns would generate backlash from these defenders. The fight isn't worth having when clowns are already declining naturally through market forces.

Third, Halloween creates a cultural release valve. Society tolerates, even celebrates, scary clowns one month per year. This contained acceptance prevents pressure from building toward outright prohibition. People who want to dress as clowns or engage with clown imagery have a socially acceptable outlet. This seasonal tolerance reduces the need for year-round acceptance.

The clown's persistence despite widespread fear reveals something about cultural change: it happens slowly, unevenly, and never completely. Traditions don't vanish overnight even when they become widely disliked. They fade gradually, persisting in diminishing forms, maintained by shrinking groups of practitioners, existing in increasingly marginal spaces.

Clowning today exists primarily in four contexts: Halloween and horror entertainment (thriving), declining traditional circuses (dying), rebranded children's entertainment (struggling), and online subcultures (fragmenting). None of these represent healthy continuation of clowning as it existed in its peak decades. All represent adaptation to a cultural environment that has fundamentally rejected what clowns were supposed to be.

The question isn't whether clowns will disappear. They will, eventually, at least in forms recognizable as traditional clowning. The question is how long the death will take. Professional organizations project their membership will drop below sustainable levels within the next decade. Circus clowns will likely persist slightly longer in small regional shows. Online clown culture will fragment into unrecognizable forms. Horror clowns will remain as long as horror remains popular.

But clowning as a profession, as a respected performance tradition, as something parents hire for parties or children enjoy without fear: that's already dead. It's been dead since Gacy, since Pennywise, since the culture collectively decided that painted smiles hide monsters. What persists now is the corpse's twitching, the final movements before the body accepts it's dead.

The clown survives not because it's wanted but because killing it completely is harder than letting it fade. No dramatic ending, no final performance, no cultural funeral. Just slow decline into irrelevance and obsolescence, maintained by shrinking numbers of people who refuse to acknowledge what's already happened.

The painted smile persists. But fewer and fewer people are wearing it, and fewer still are smiling back.

Chapter Thirteen

The Future of the Killer Clown

The killer clown is not disappearing. If anything, it's evolving, adapting to new technologies and cultural anxieties, finding new ways to terrify in an era when traditional scares have lost their impact through overexposure. The future of the killer clown lies not in circuses or birthday parties but in digital spaces, artificial intelligence, and the blurring line between virtual and real.

Deepfake technology has already been used to create unsettling clown content. Videos show clowns with faces that move in impossible ways, expressions that shift too quickly, smiles that stretch beyond human capability. These aren't traditional special effects but AI-generated imagery that exists in the uncanny valley between real and fake. The viewer knows something is wrong but cannot pinpoint exactly what. The brain recognizes the impossibility while the eyes insist it's seeing something real.

This technology will only improve. Within years, we'll have the ability to generate photorealistic videos of clowns doing anything, appearing anywhere, tailored to individual fears based on data harvesting and psychological profiling. Imagine receiving a video of a clown standing outside your actual house, the image generated using street view data and AI, personalized to include details only you would recognize. The clown knows your address. The clown knows what your house looks like. The clown is coming for you specifically.

Virtual reality offers another frontier for clown horror. Current VR horror experiences featuring clowns are crude but effective, trapping users in environments where clowns can approach from any direction, invade personal space in ways that feel viscerally real despite being digital. As VR technology improves, these experiences will become increasingly indistinguishable from reality. The brain will respond to virtual clowns the same way it responds to physical ones, triggering genuine fear responses.

Augmented reality presents even more disturbing possibilities. AR overlays digital content onto the real world through phone screens or glasses. Imagine walking down your street and seeing, through your phone, a clown standing on the corner that isn't physically there but appears real through your screen. Other people using the same app see it too. Is it there or not? The question becomes meaningless when the digital and physical are inseparably merged.

Gaming has already embraced clown horror extensively, but future developments will make these experiences more immersive and psychologically sophisticated. AI-driven clown antagonists that learn from player behavior, adapting their tactics to exploit individual fears and weaknesses. Clowns that remember previous encounters across gaming sessions, building long-term psychological campaigns against players. Horror that persists beyond the game itself, with clowns sending messages to players' phones, appearing in other applications, breaking the boundary between game world and real world.

Artificial intelligence is already being used to generate clown images, stories, and videos. Current AI-generated clown content tends toward the bizarre and surreal, but the technology is improving rapidly. Soon AI will be able to generate horror content more effectively than human creators can, tailoring it to individual psychological profiles, testing infinite variations to find what triggers the strongest fear responses, optimizing for maximum psychological impact.

The combination of these technologies creates possibilities for clown horror that are genuinely disturbing to contemplate. Personalized horror experiences generated by AI, delivered through AR or VR, shared virally through social media. The killer clown of the future won't be a person in a costume. It will be a distributed digital phenomenon that exists simultaneously everywhere and nowhere, impossible to escape or combat through traditional means.

Younger generations interact with clown horror differently than their parents did. For millennials, Pennywise and the Joker were revelations, transforming how they saw clowns. For Generation Z and younger, clowns have always been scary. They have no memory of clowns as purely wholesome entertainment. The killer clown is the only clown they've ever known.

This creates interesting dynamics. The transgression that gave killer clowns their power (violating the expectation of wholesome entertainment) no longer exists for younger audiences. Clowns aren't scary because they corrupt innocence; they're scary because they've always been presented as scary. This might eventually diminish their impact as the element of violated expectations disappears.

Alternatively, it might create a new form of fear, one based not on violated expectations but on inherited cultural trauma. These younger audiences fear clowns because their parents feared clowns, because the culture tells them clowns are frightening, because every representation they've encountered has reinforced this message. The fear becomes detached from any specific reason, becoming almost instinctual, a cultural inheritance passed down like genetic memory.

Marketing and advertising have begun weaponizing clown imagery in ways that blur the line between promotion and psychological attack. Horror films use clown imagery in ad campaigns designed to go viral through fear rather than appeal. These campaigns don't try to make the film look entertaining; they try to make the clown look genuinely threatening, banking on coulrophobia to generate attention and controversy.

Some campaigns have gone further, creating fake social media accounts for fictional clowns, having them interact with real users, blurring the line between promotional material and actual threat. Users cannot be certain whether the clown account messaging them is marketing or harassment. The ambiguity is intentional, designed to maximize engagement through uncertainty and fear.

This weaponization will only increase. In an attention economy where fear drives engagement as effectively as any positive emotion, clowns represent a ready-made tool for capturing attention. Brands, creators, and bad actors will continue deploying clown imagery to trigger responses, to go viral, to dominate conversations. The clown becomes a psychological weapon, optimized not for entertainment but for maximum impact on human emotional circuitry.

The creator economy on platforms like TikTok, YouTube, and Instagram has spawned a new genre of clown content that exists in moral and artistic gray areas. Creators dress as disturbing clowns and film themselves in public spaces, recording the reactions of unsuspecting people. These videos generate millions of views because they capture genuine fear responses. People scream, run, sometimes become aggressive. The creators frame this as entertainment, as harmless pranks, but the psychological impact on victims is real.

This trend will expand as platforms continue rewarding engagement regardless of how that engagement is generated. Creators will develop more sophisticated and disturbing approaches, using better costumes, more strategic locations, coordinating with other creators for larger scale events. The line between content creation and public menace will become increasingly difficult to define.

Law enforcement faces challenges adapting to these new forms of clown-related behavior. Is someone in a clown costume filming reactions committing a crime? Often no, unless they make specific threats or physically touch people. But they're clearly causing distress, creating public disruptions, potentially traumatizing people with coulrophobia. Existing laws don't adequately address this behavior, leaving police unable to intervene effectively even when the behavior is obviously harmful.

New legislation may emerge to address this gap, but creating laws that prohibit disturbing behavior while respecting free expression is legally complex. Any law too broadly written will face constitutional challenges. Too narrow and it becomes ineffective. The legal system will struggle to keep pace with evolving forms of clown-based harassment and terror.

Therapeutic approaches to coulrophobia will need to evolve as well. Traditional exposure therapy becomes complicated when the feared stimulus is legitimately dangerous in some contexts. Exposing someone to clowns to reduce their fear makes sense if clowns are harmless. But if some clowns genuinely pose threats (using costumes to conceal identity while engaging in harassment or worse), then fear becomes a rational protective response that shouldn't be eliminated.

Future therapy may focus less on eliminating fear of clowns and more on helping people distinguish between threatening and non-threatening clown encounters. This requires developing new frameworks for assessment that don't currently exist. How do you tell the difference between a harmless performer and a predator when both wear the same costume? The answer may be that you can't, and therapy should help people accept and manage that uncertainty rather than overcome it.

The horror genre will continue mining clown imagery, but diminishing returns are inevitable. Each new killer clown film or game or story must compete with decades of predecessors. Innovation becomes harder. Audiences become desensitized. What shocked viewers in the 1980s barely registers now. Future clown horror will need to find new angles, new combinations of elements, new ways to make the familiar frightening again.

Some creators are moving toward meta-horror that acknowledges the cultural saturation of killer clowns and plays with audience expectations. Horror that's aware the audience has seen it all before, that uses familiarity as part of the scare, that subverts expectations precisely because those expectations have been so firmly established. This approach has limits but represents one possible evolution.

Another direction is extreme intensity, pushing boundaries of graphic violence and psychological torture to generate responses in audiences numbed by decades of horror content. The "Terrifier" films represent this approach, using Art the Clown to deliver violence so extreme it breaks through desensitization. Future iterations will likely go further, testing how much audiences can tolerate before the content becomes genuinely unwatchable rather than entertainingly horrifying.

International markets present interesting possibilities for clown horror evolution. Western cultural associations between clowns and terror are not universal. Some cultures have different performance traditions, different entertainment histories, different relationships with masked performers. As global media markets integrate, these different cultural contexts will produce new variations on killer clown themes, hybridizing Western tropes with local traditions and fears.

Japanese horror has already produced distinctive takes on clown-adjacent imagery through their own performance traditions. Future horror from other regions may similarly adapt the killer clown archetype to local contexts, creating variations that feel fresh to Western audiences while resonating with local cultural anxieties.

Climate change and societal collapse anxieties may influence how clowns are used symbolically in future horror. The clown as symbol of failed civilization, of social systems breaking down, of the performance of normalcy continuing while everything burns. This metaphorical use could give new depth to clown horror, making it about larger cultural fears rather than just the clown itself.

Political movements and protests will likely continue appropriating clown imagery, using it to mock authority, to remain anonymous, to project chaos and disruption. This use reinforces the association between clowns and societal breakdown, feeding back into horror applications. Real-world political clowns and fictional horror clowns will continue influencing each other in recursive loops.

The most disturbing possibility is that real-world violence may increasingly involve clown imagery not coincidentally but deliberately. People planning attacks or harassment campaigns using clown costumes specifically because of the cultural associations, because of the fear the imagery generates, because they've consumed the horror media and understood its effectiveness. The killer clown stops being entirely fictional and becomes a template that some people choose to enact.

This has already happened in limited ways with various attacks and threats involving clown costumes or imagery. Future incidents may be more common and more explicitly inspired by fictional killer clowns. The cultural creation feeds back into reality, creating actual monsters based on the imagined ones.

Technology companies will face pressure to moderate clown-related content but will resist doing so because fear-based content drives engagement and profits. Platforms may implement minimal age restrictions or warning labels but will avoid aggressive moderation that would reduce viral spread. The economic incentives favor allowing disturbing clown content to proliferate.

Educational systems may eventually need to address coulrophobia as a legitimate concern affecting significant portions of the student population. School counselors already encounter students with severe clown fears. As the percentage increases, schools may develop specific protocols, eliminate clown-related imagery from educational materials, train staff on how to handle coulrophobic reactions.

This institutional acknowledgment would represent the final phase of cultural transformation: clowns not just feared by individuals but recognized by institutions as legitimate sources of distress requiring accommodation. At that point, the battle is over. Clowns will have completed their journey from entertainers to officially recognized threats.

The future of the killer clown is not one thing but many things simultaneously. Digital evolution, cultural evolution, technological weaponization, globalized hybridization, increasingly extreme horror content, real-world violence borrowing fictional imagery, institutional recognition of coulrophobia as legitimate. All of these will happen in parallel, creating a future where clowns are more terrifying, more pervasive, and more impossible to escape than they've ever been.

The painted smile won't fade. It will multiply, appearing on screens and in streets, in games and in nightmares, generated by algorithms and worn by people with unknowable intentions. The future of the killer clown is one where the boundary between real and fake dissolves completely, where fear becomes indistinguishable from marketing, where the costume that once brought joy now exists solely to terrify.

And there's no going back.

Postword: When the Paint Dries

The clown has always had permission to hurt you.

That's the part we don't talk about enough. The jester could mock the condemned man on his way to execution. The circus clown could single you out of the crowd, make you the butt of the joke, and humiliate you in front of hundreds of people. The birthday party clown could terrify your child, invade their space, ignore their tears, and you were expected to smile and pay for the privilege. The clown had social license to violate boundaries, to disrespect, to mock, and you had no recourse.

Fight back, and you're the problem. You're uptight. You can't take a joke. You're ruining everyone else's fun. The clown makes you the target and the crowd laughs, and if you object, the laughter turns on you even harder. You're trapped. The clown can do anything to you and you must accept it with a smile, because challenging a clown means challenging the performance itself, means rejecting the social contract that says this is all in good fun.

Except it's not fun. Not for the target. The clown's comedy often depends on someone else's humiliation, discomfort, or fear. Someone has to be the fool, the victim, the object of mockery. And once the clown selects you, there's no escape without social cost. You cannot fight back. You cannot defend yourself. You can only endure while everyone around you laughs at your distress.

This is why coulrophobia is justified. The fear isn't irrational. It's a rational response to a figure that has social permission to harm you while you have no permission to defend yourself. The clown can mock, invade, terrify, humiliate, and society protects the clown, not you. Your fear, your anger, your discomfort: all of this is dismissed as your failure to appreciate entertainment.

Think about the historical jester, standing before a man who's been sentenced to death, making jokes about his fate while the crowd roars with laughter. The condemned man cannot respond. He's about to die. The jester mocks his final moments, and this is considered acceptable, even laudable. The jester is entertaining the crowd. The dying man's dignity is irrelevant.

Or consider the child at a birthday party, crying because the clown won't leave them alone. The clown keeps approaching, keeps trying to engage, keeps invading the child's space despite obvious distress. The adults laugh nervously. "It's just a clown," they say. "Don't be scared." The child's fear is treated as unreasonable, something to be overcome rather than respected. The clown's behavior, the actual cause of the distress, is never questioned.

This dynamic has always been present, but we've spent centuries pretending it was harmless. We told ourselves that clowns brought joy, that their boundary violations were innocent fun, that being selected as the target of their mockery was an honor or at least not genuinely harmful. We lied to ourselves because the alternative was acknowledging that we'd given cultural permission for a form of sanctioned cruelty.

The killer clown in horror doesn't pervert something innocent. It reveals what was always there. The violation, the mockery, the powerlessness: these elements were always part of what clowns did. Horror just stopped pretending that these things were funny. The clown that humiliates you at a party and the clown that murders you in a horror film operate on the same principle. You have no power. The clown has all of it. And no one will help you.

This is the truth we've finally acknowledged. The cultural transformation of clowns from entertainers to monsters isn't corruption of innocence. It's recognition of what clowns actually were: figures with social permission to harm without consequence, to violate without punishment, to mock without response. We granted them this power thinking it was contained by performance, by entertainment, by the understanding that it was all just fun.

But power doesn't stay contained. Permission to violate boundaries "as a joke" is still permission to violate boundaries. The target's distress doesn't become less real because everyone else is laughing. The humiliation doesn't hurt less because it's supposedly entertainment. And the fear doesn't become irrational just because the figure causing it wears a funny costume.

We created the killer clown by finally admitting what the clown always was: a figure with power over you that you cannot challenge, that can hurt you while everyone watches and laughs, that operates outside the normal rules of social interaction. The horror version just makes explicit what was always implicit. The clown could always hurt you. Now it does so honestly, without pretending the pain is entertainment.

The painted smile was never friendly. It was a warning that normal rules don't apply here, that your discomfort doesn't matter, that the performance will continue regardless of how you feel. The costume was never innocent. It marked someone who had permission to do things that would be unacceptable from anyone else. The bells and the makeup and the oversized shoes: all of it signaled that this person could violate your boundaries, and you had to accept it.

Your fear is not weakness. Your discomfort is not failure. Your instinct to avoid clowns, to protect your children from them, to feel anxiety when they approach: all of this is appropriate response to a genuine threat. Not the threat of physical violence necessarily, but the threat of powerlessness, of being made the target of mockery you cannot challenge, of having your boundaries violated while being told you should enjoy it.

The clown's reign is ending not because we've become oversensitive or lost our sense of humor. It's ending because we've finally stopped accepting the premise that some people should have permission to hurt others for entertainment. The social contract that protected clowns has broken down. We no longer agree that boundary violation is acceptable when performed by someone in costume. We no longer pretend that mockery stops being cruel just because it's presented as comedy.

This is progress, not loss. We haven't destroyed something beautiful. We've recognized something ugly that we'd been trained not to see. The clown didn't fall from grace. We simply stopped granting it special status, stopped giving it permission to do harm, stopped protecting the performance at the expense of the victims.

The killer clown is the clown without social protection, without the lie that its violations are entertainment, without the pretense that the smile means anything other than the power to hurt you while you're powerless to respond. It's the truth we've been avoiding for centuries: the clown was always the monster.

The paint is drying. The performance is ending. The social permission has been revoked. And what remains when you strip away the pretense is exactly what we always feared it was.

A predator in costume. A bully with bells. A figure that hurts you and calls it fun.

The only difference now is that we've stopped laughing.

www.ingramcontent.com/pod-product-compliance
Lightning Source LLC
LaVergne TN
LVHW022106200926
848481LV00003B/1076
9798233684074